Seashells

A Still Life Coloring Book

Illustrations by
Sue-Jen Song

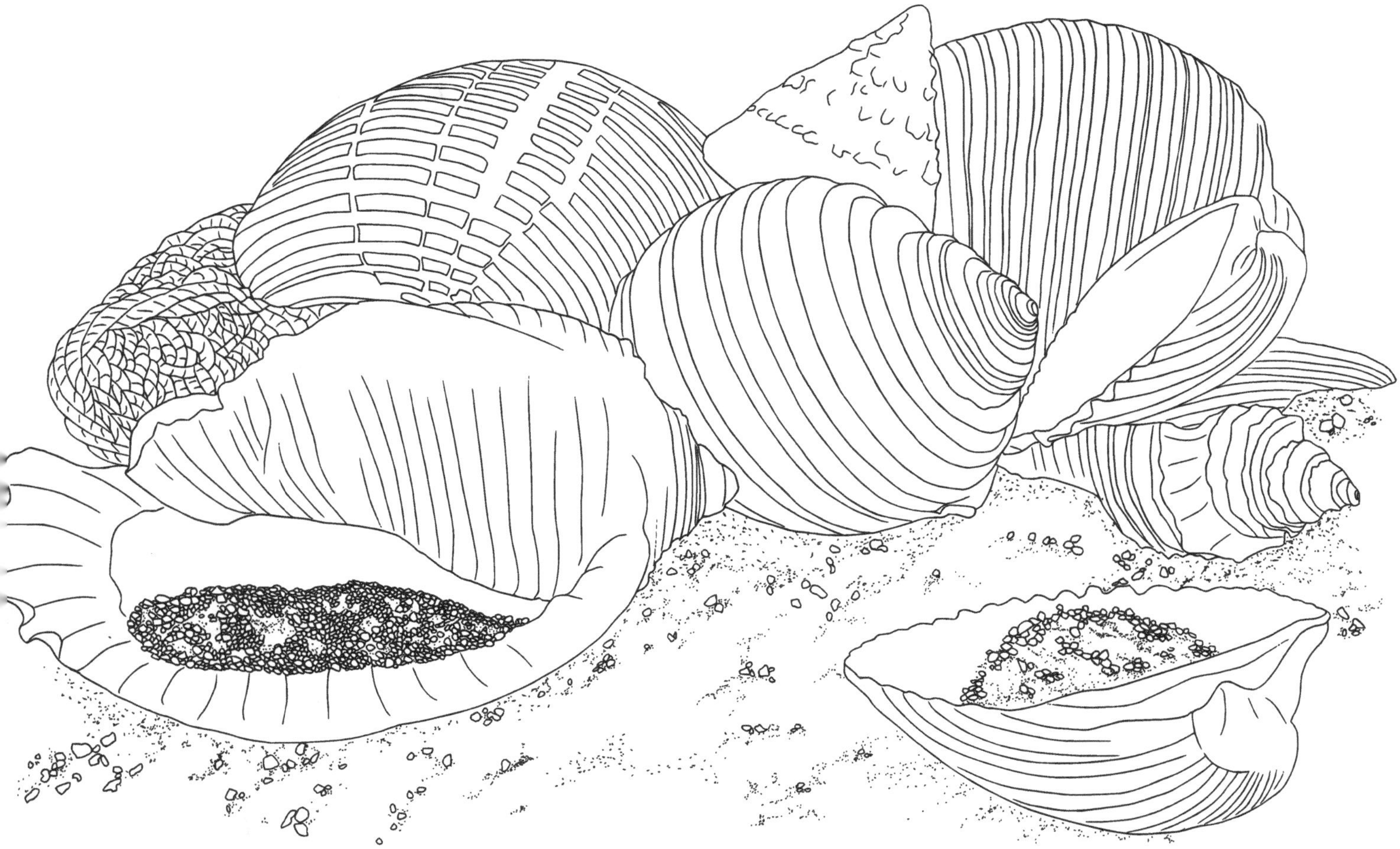

ISBN: 978-1983535444
First Edition

Printed by CreateSpace, An Amazon.com
Company

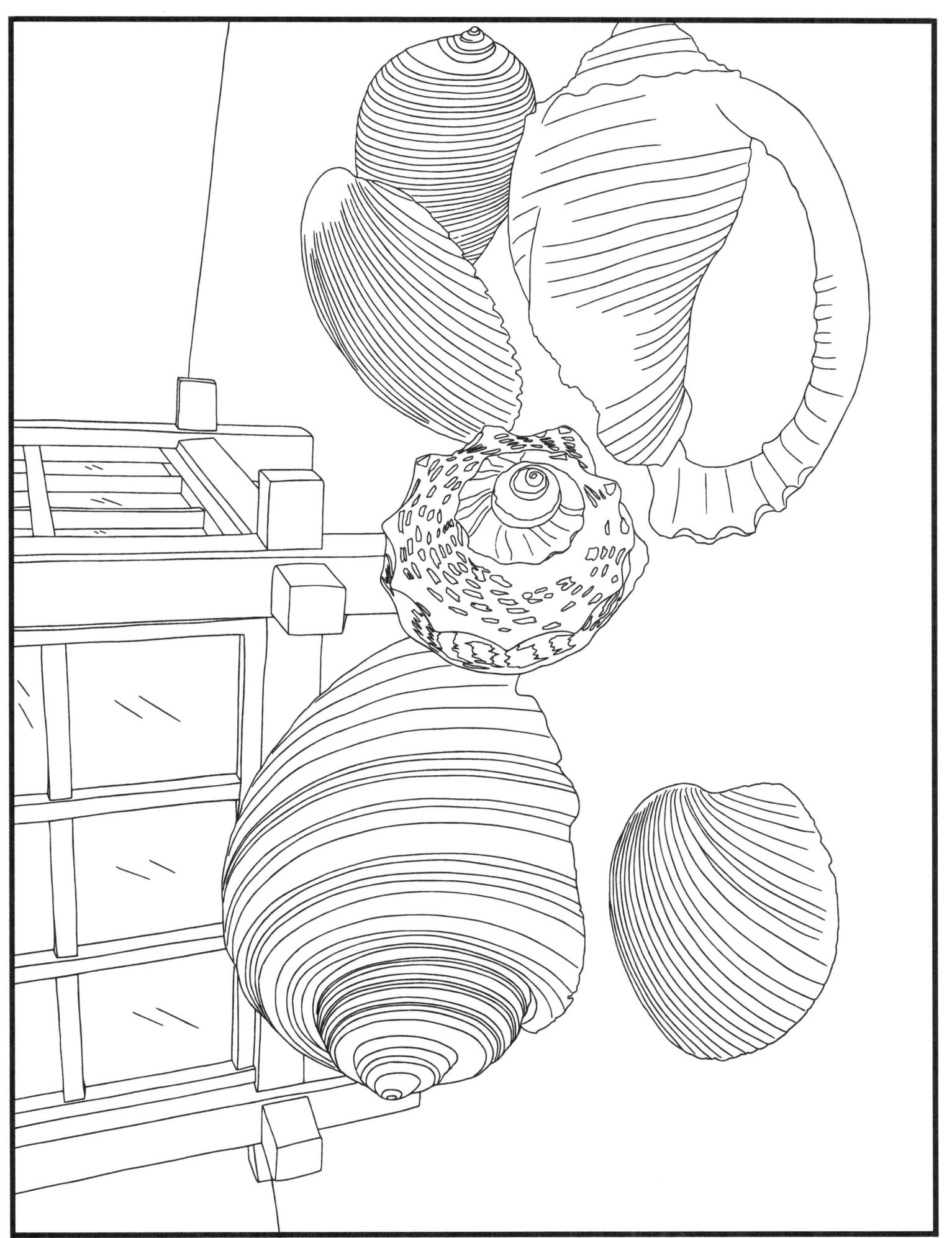

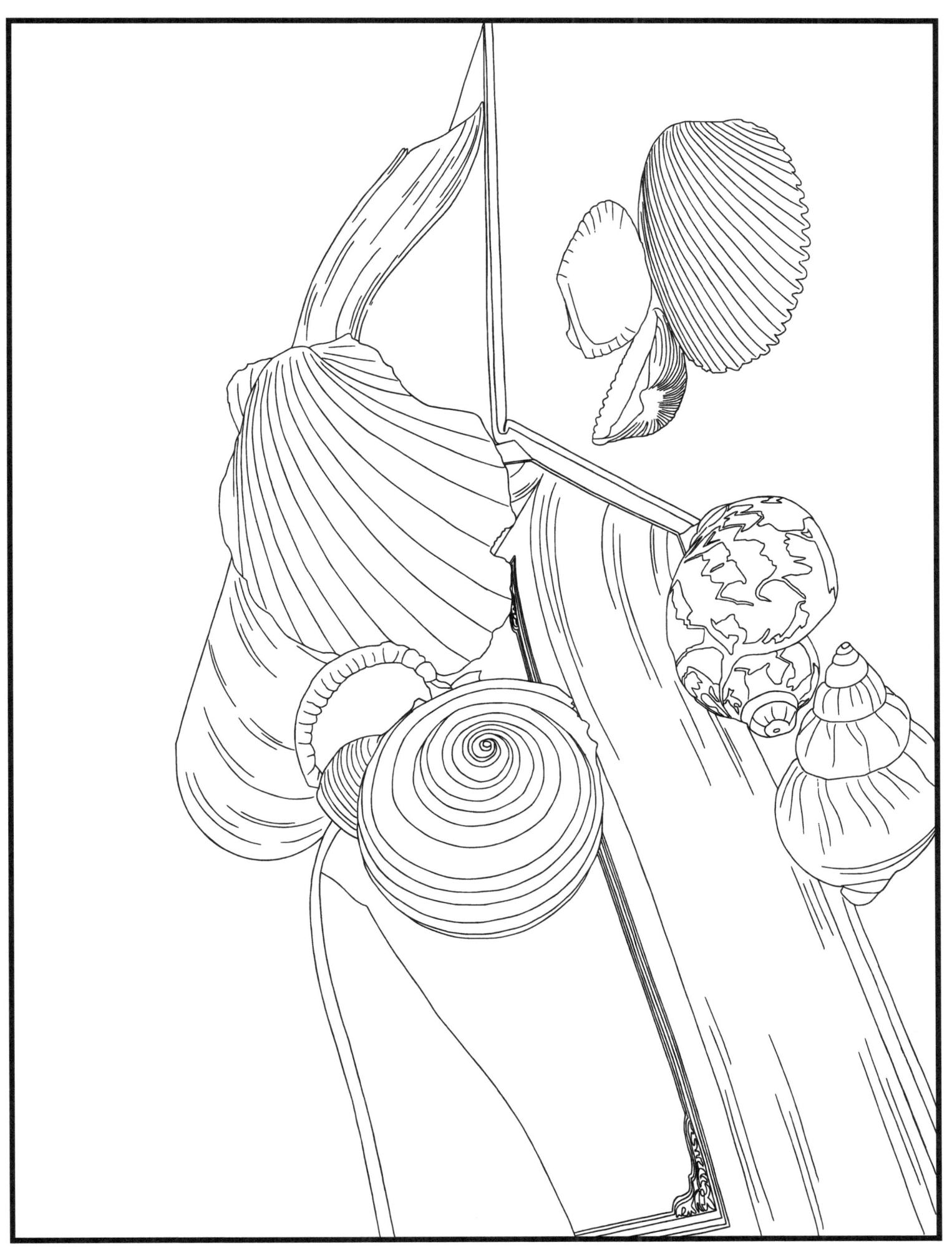

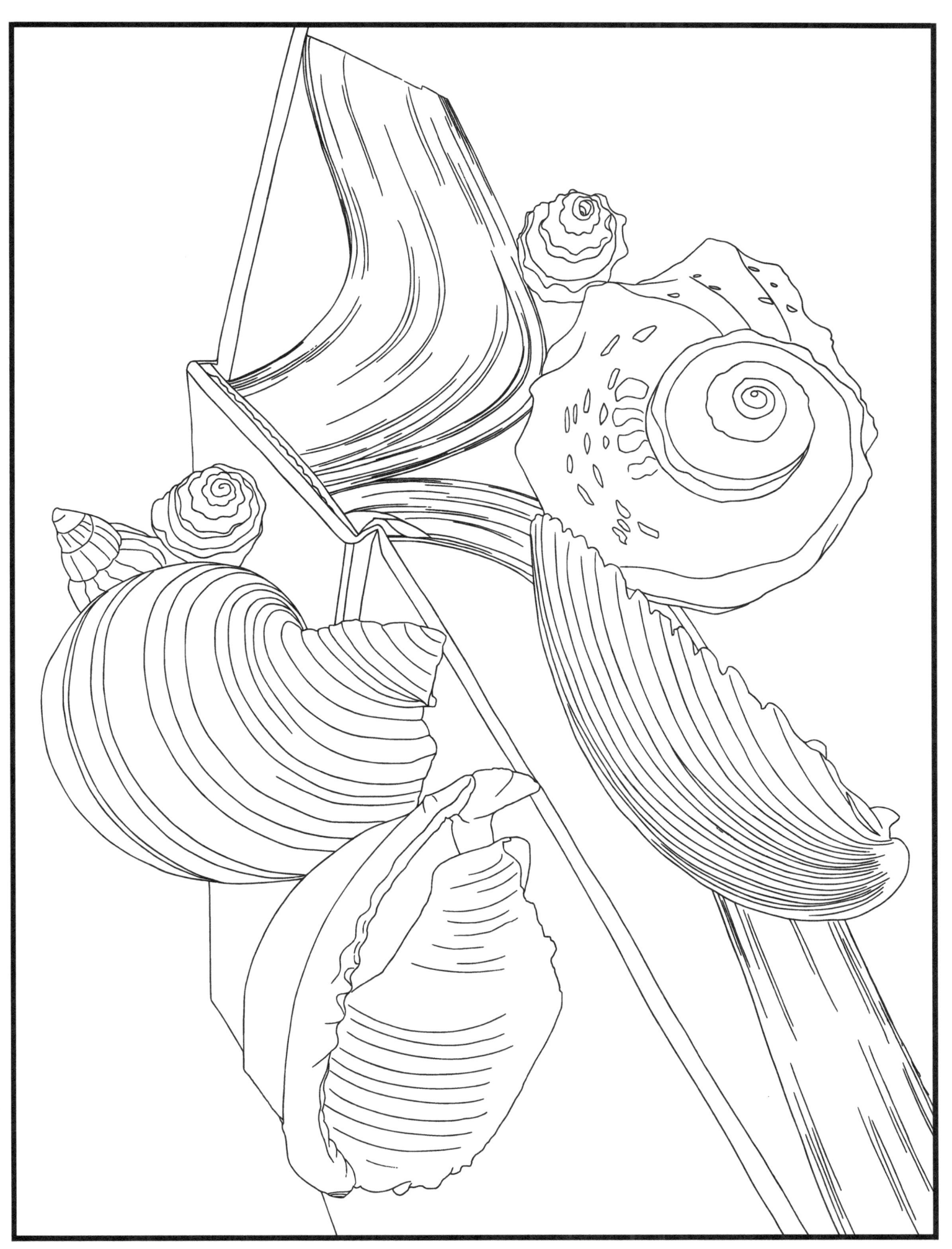

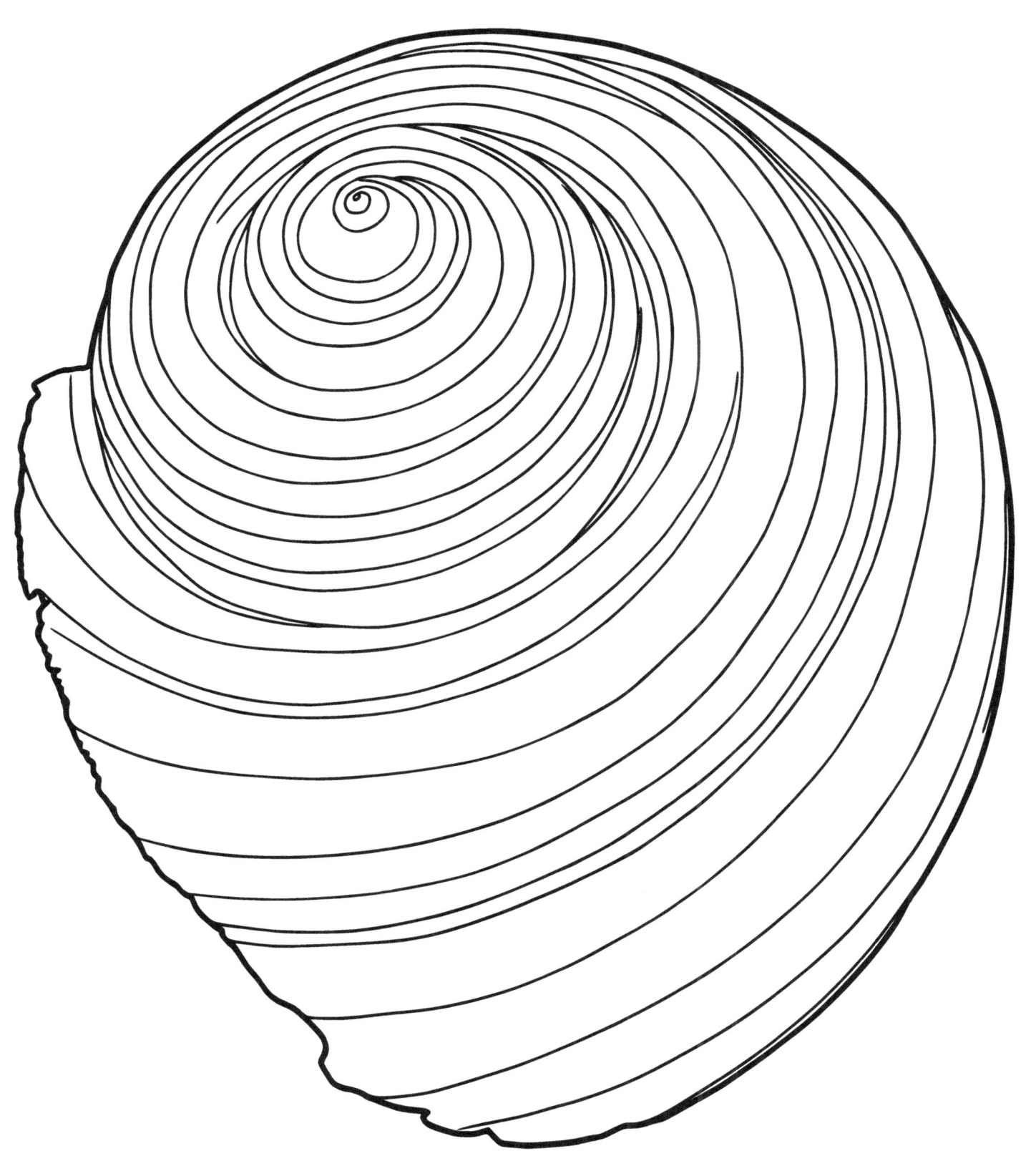

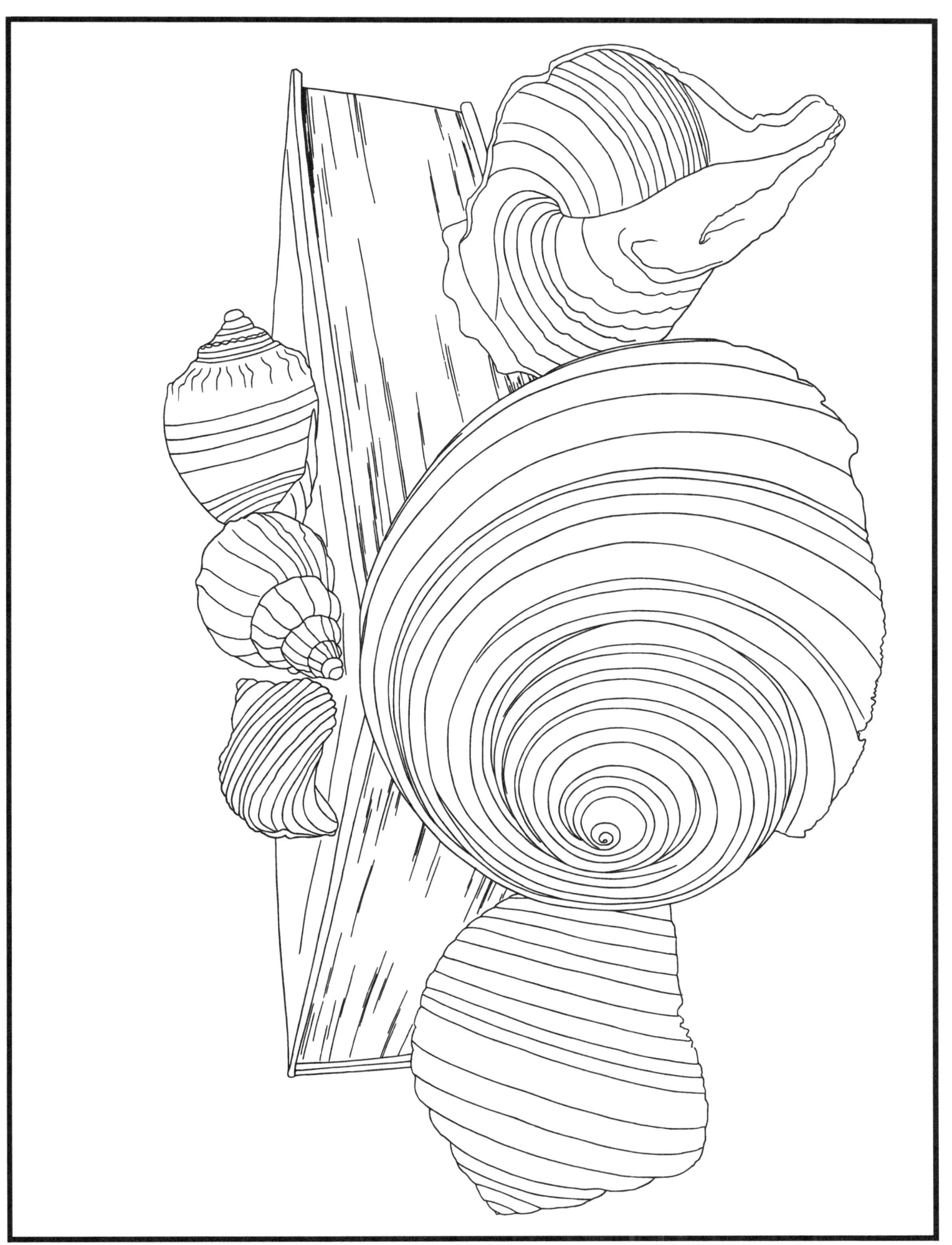

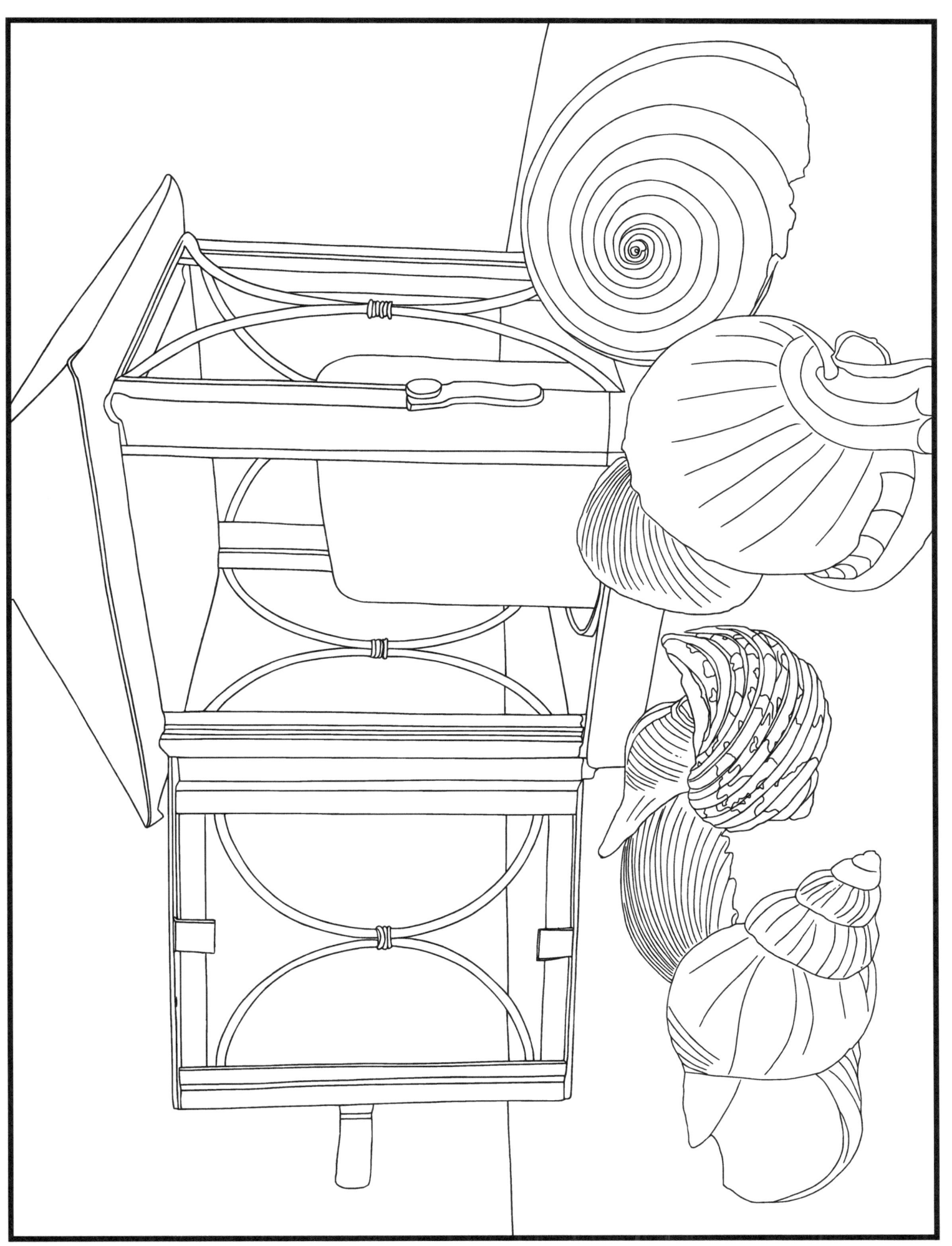

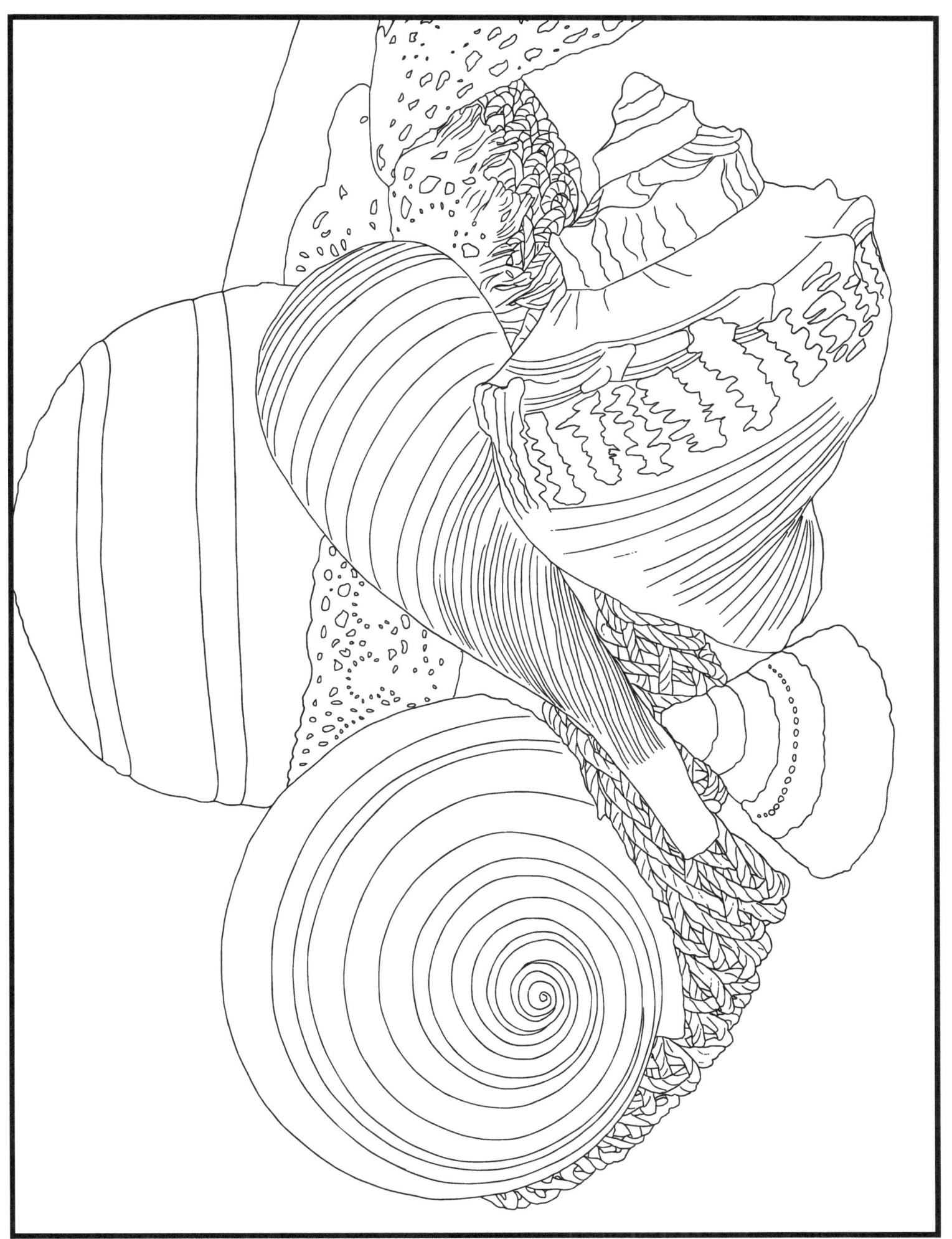

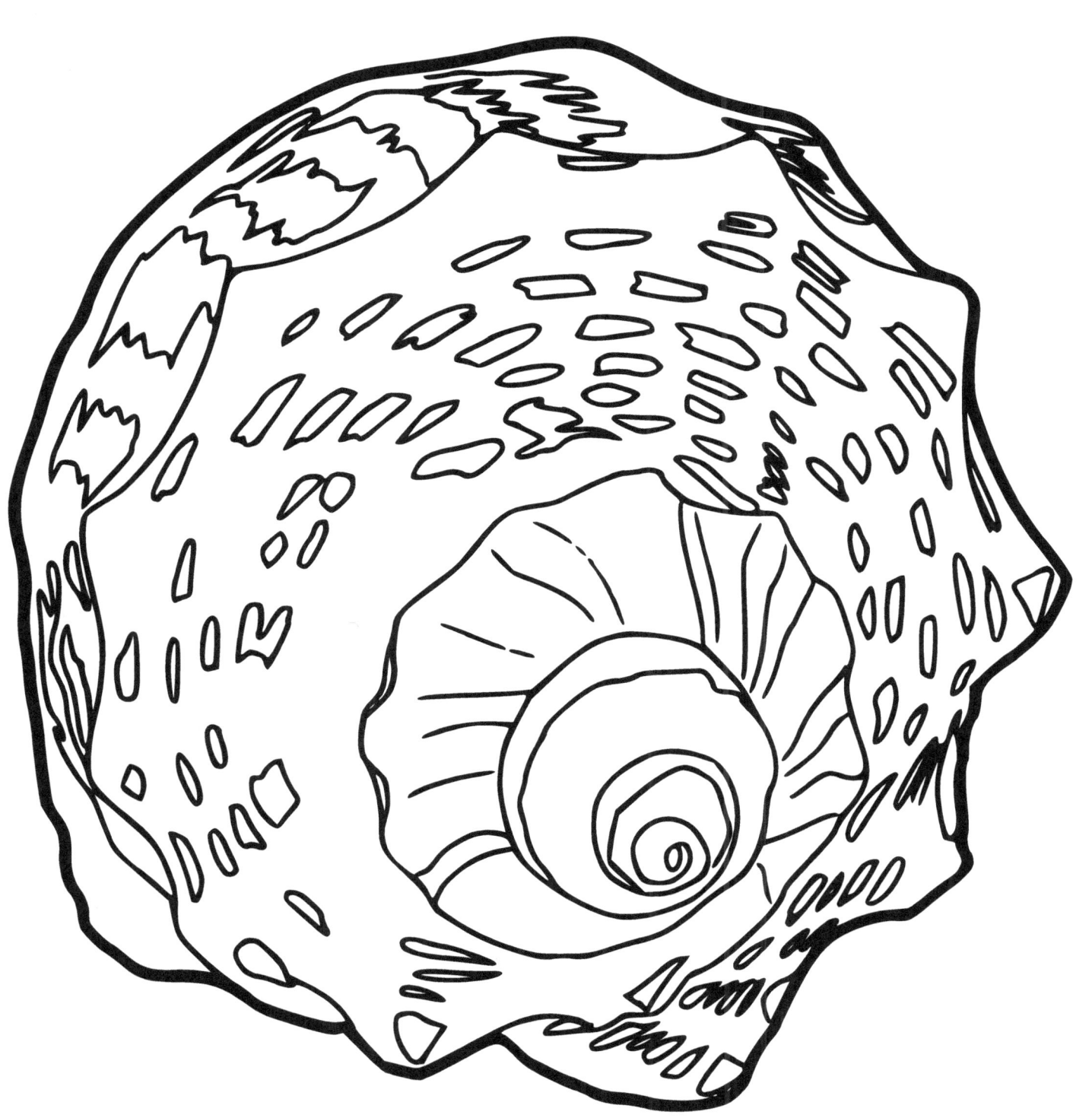

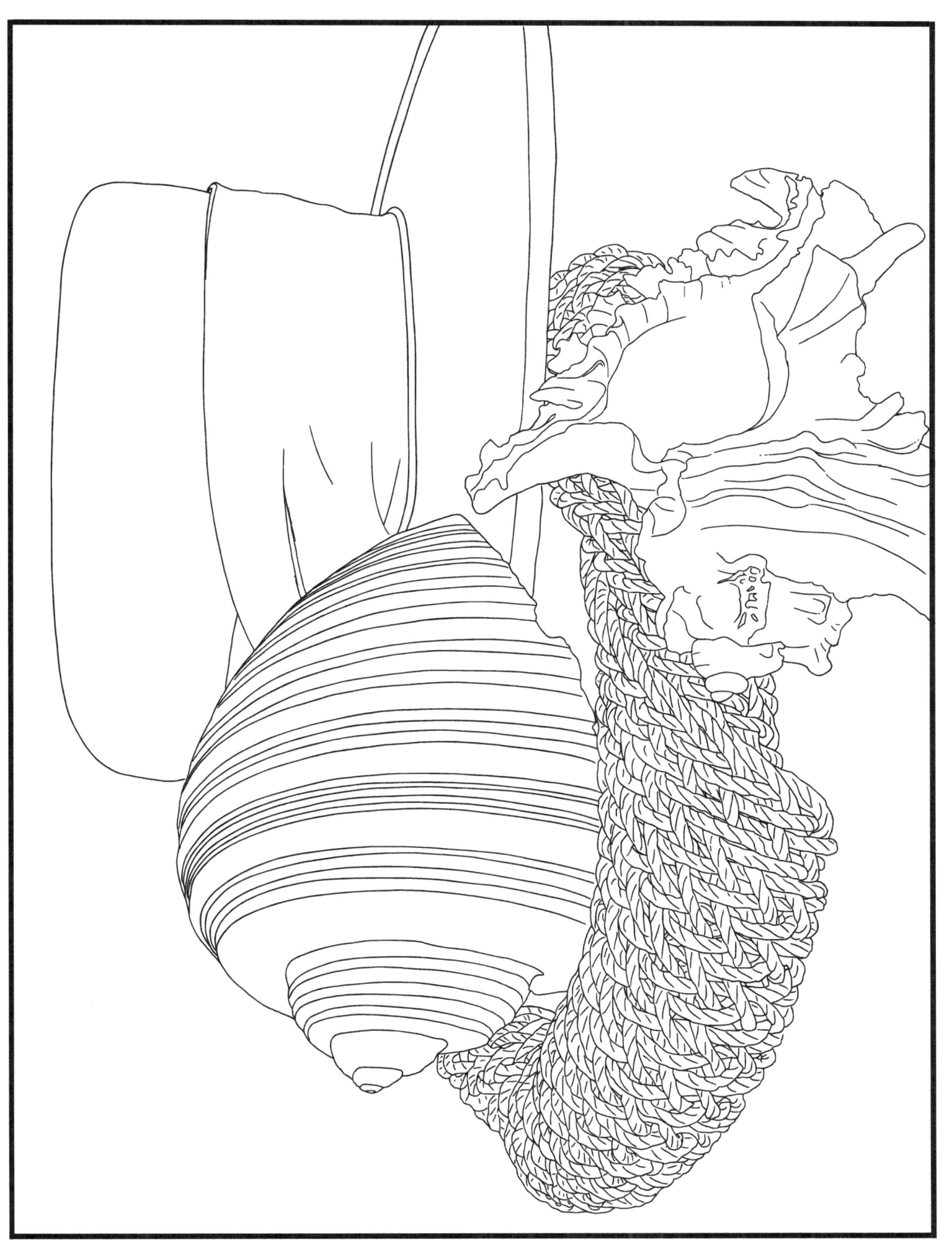

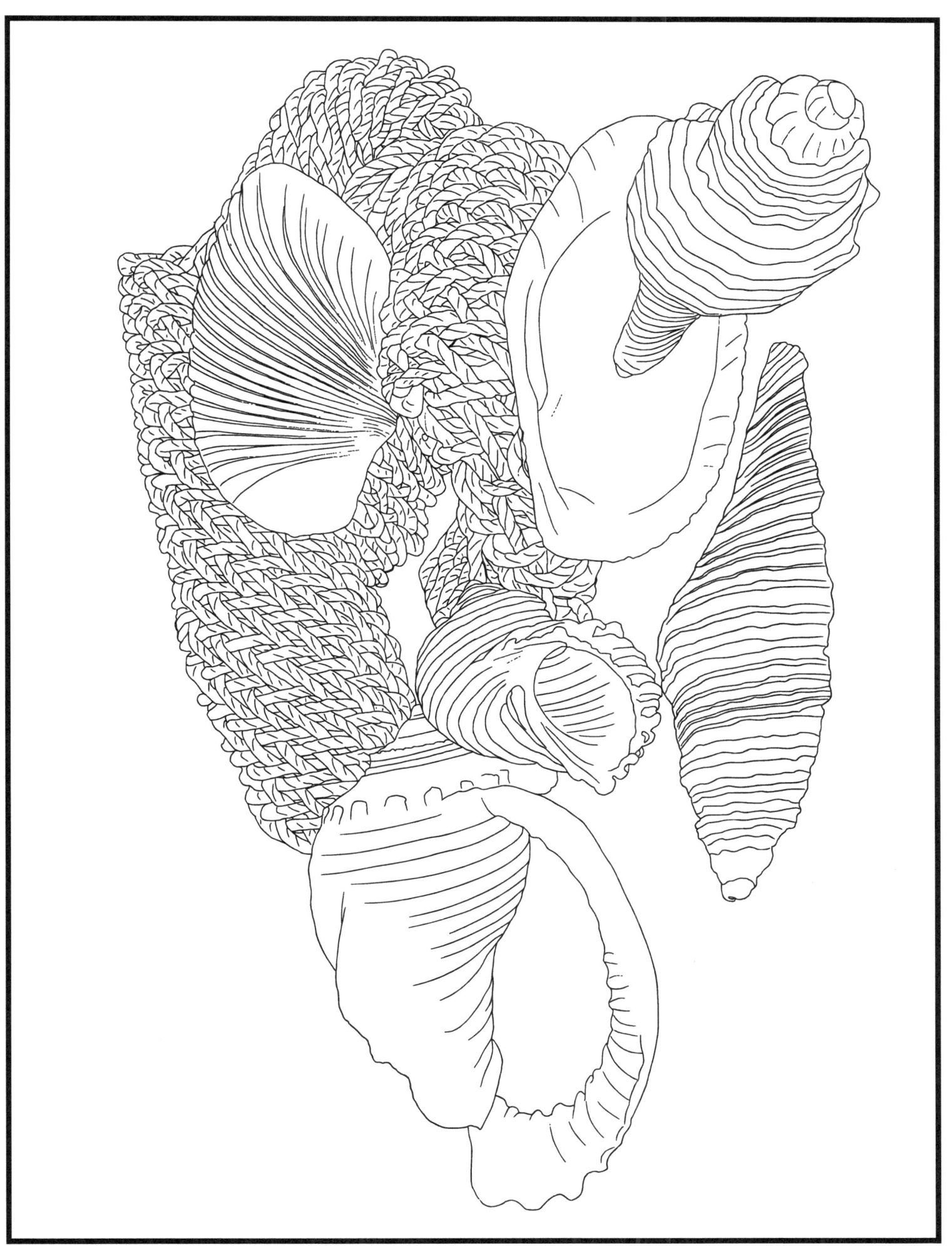

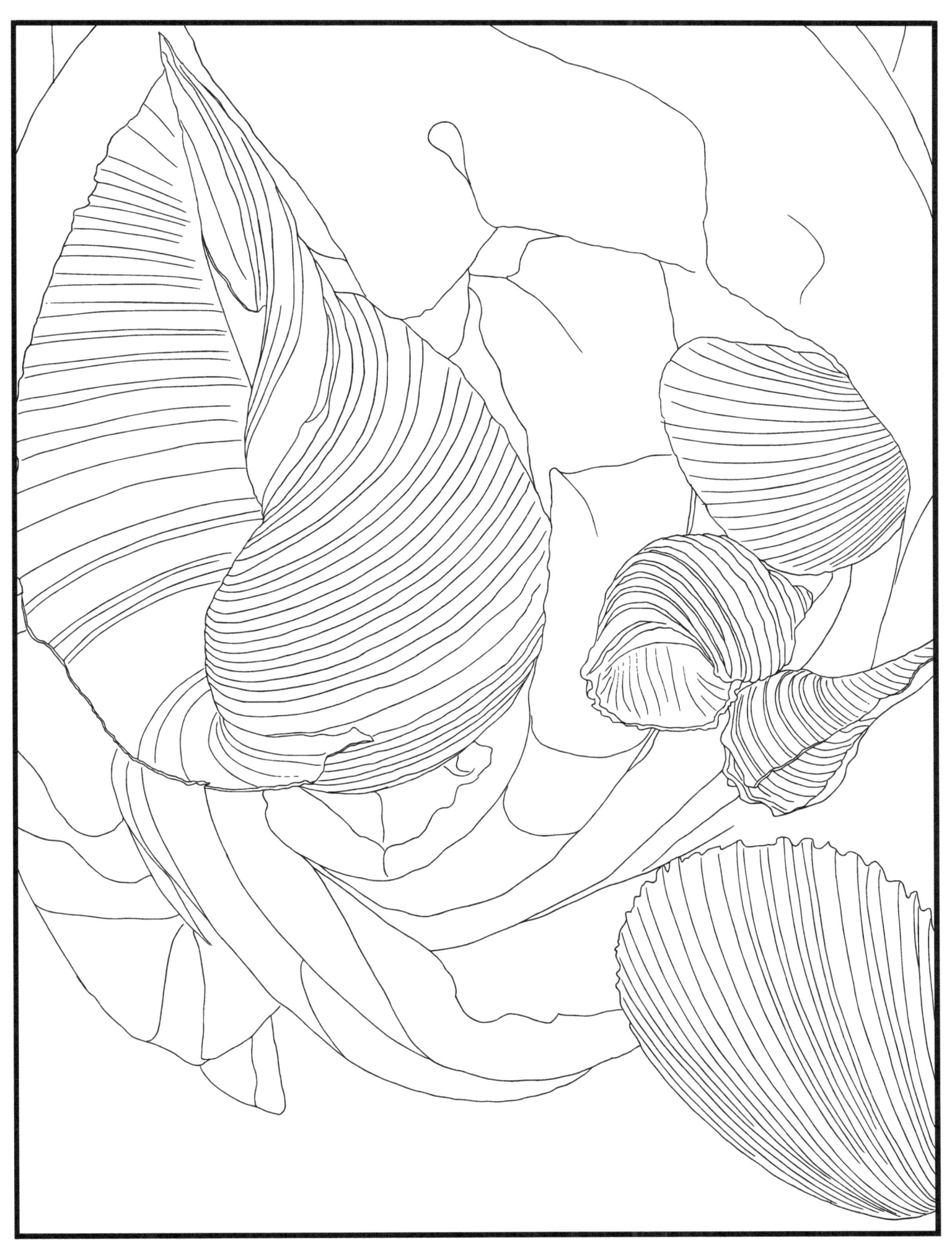

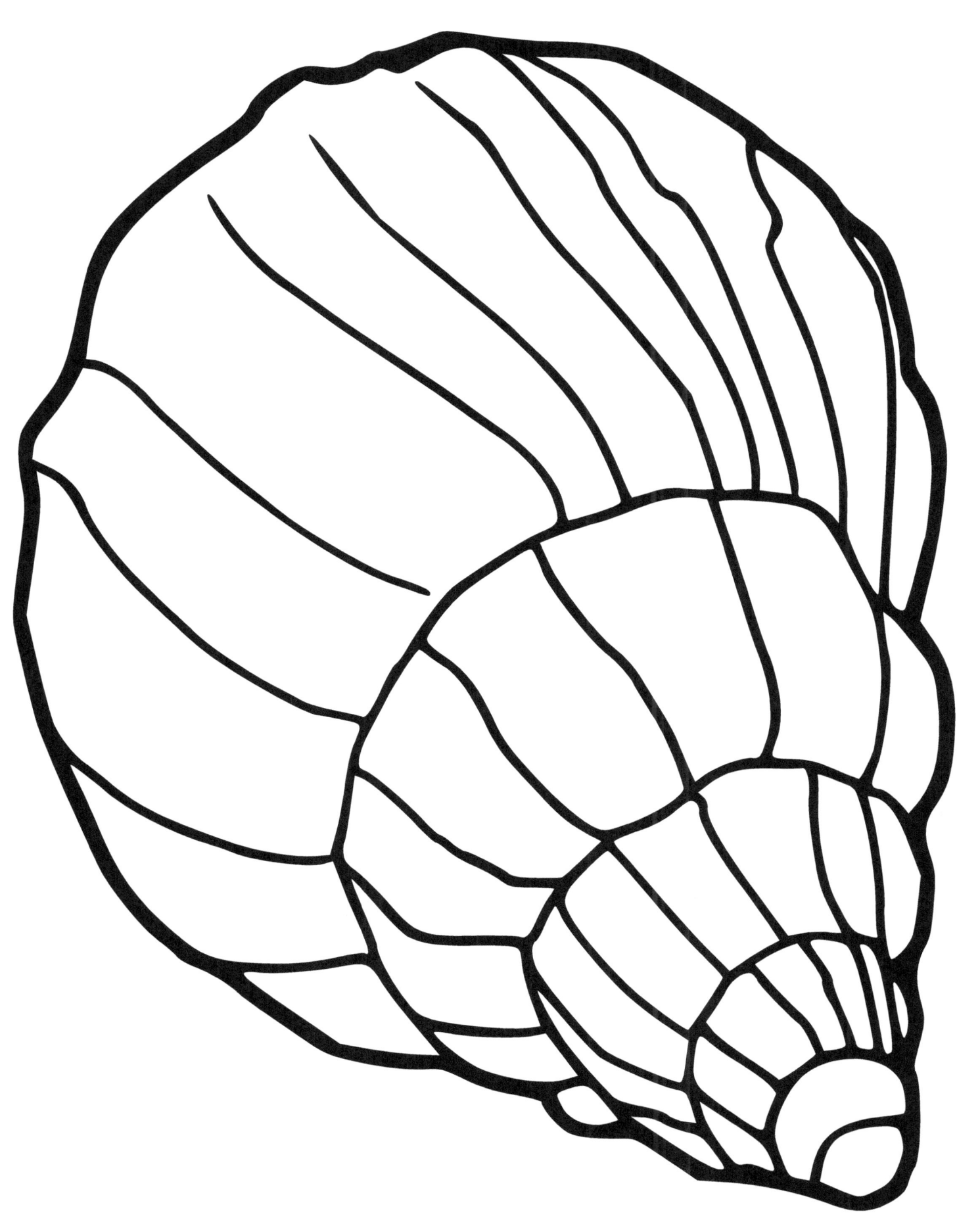

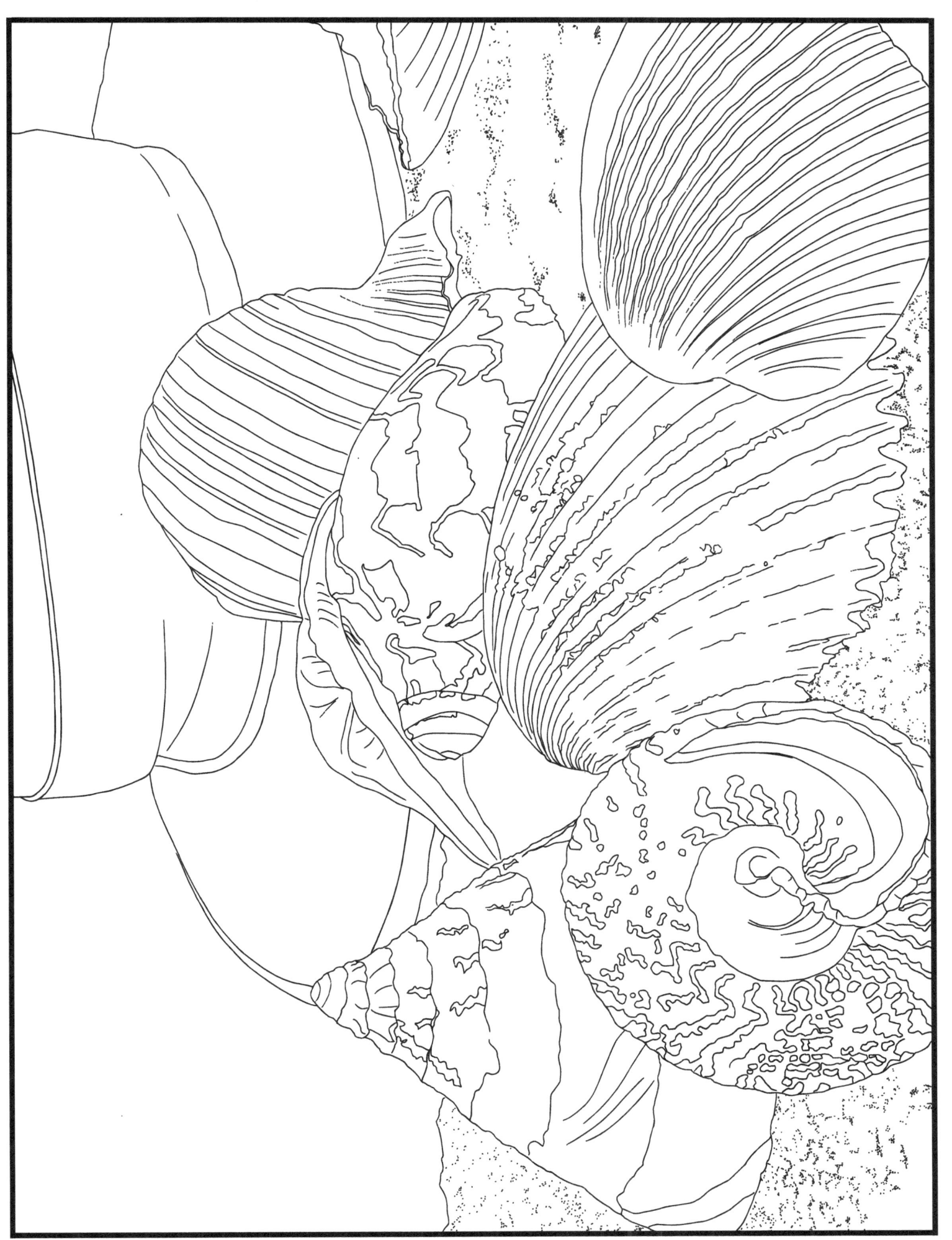

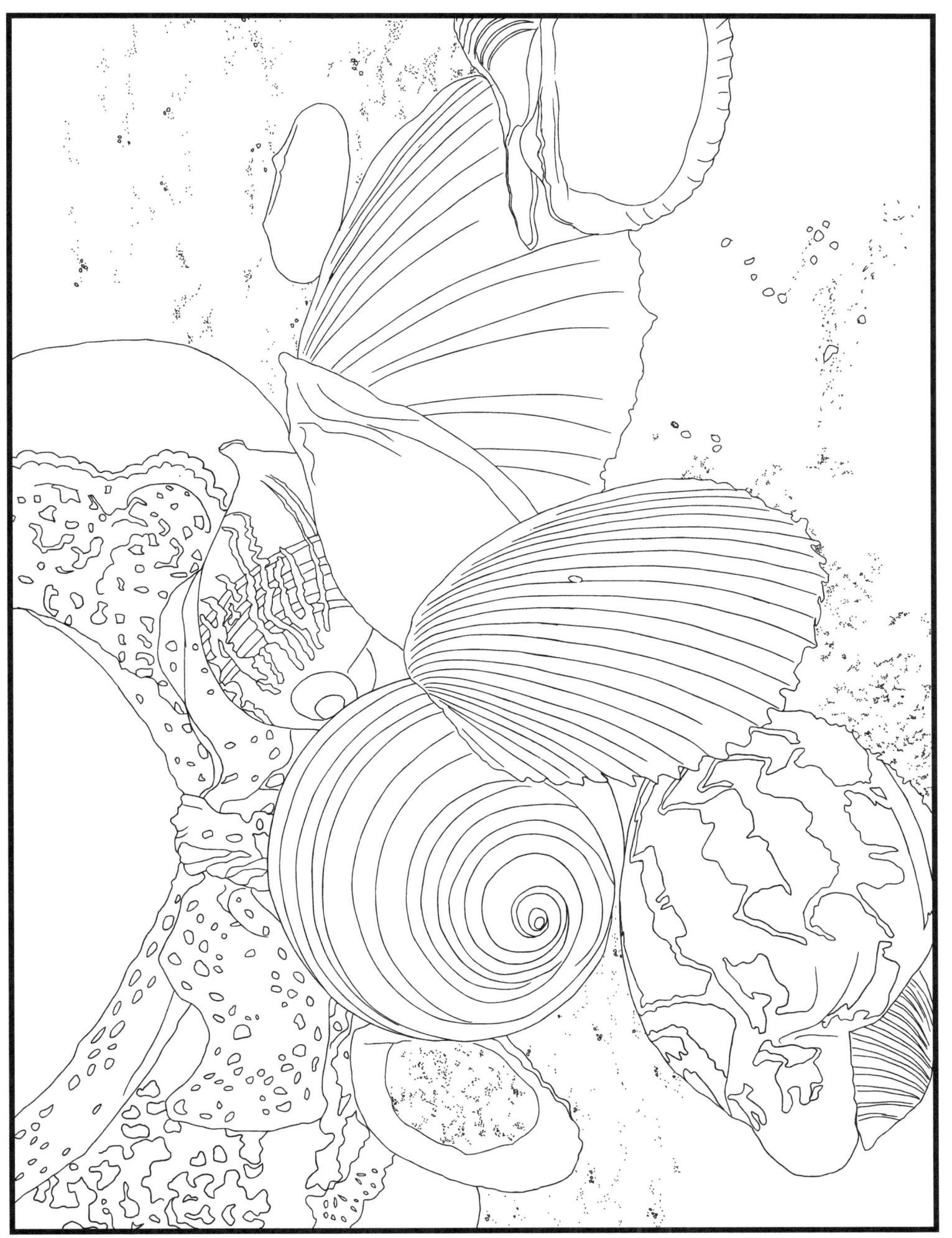

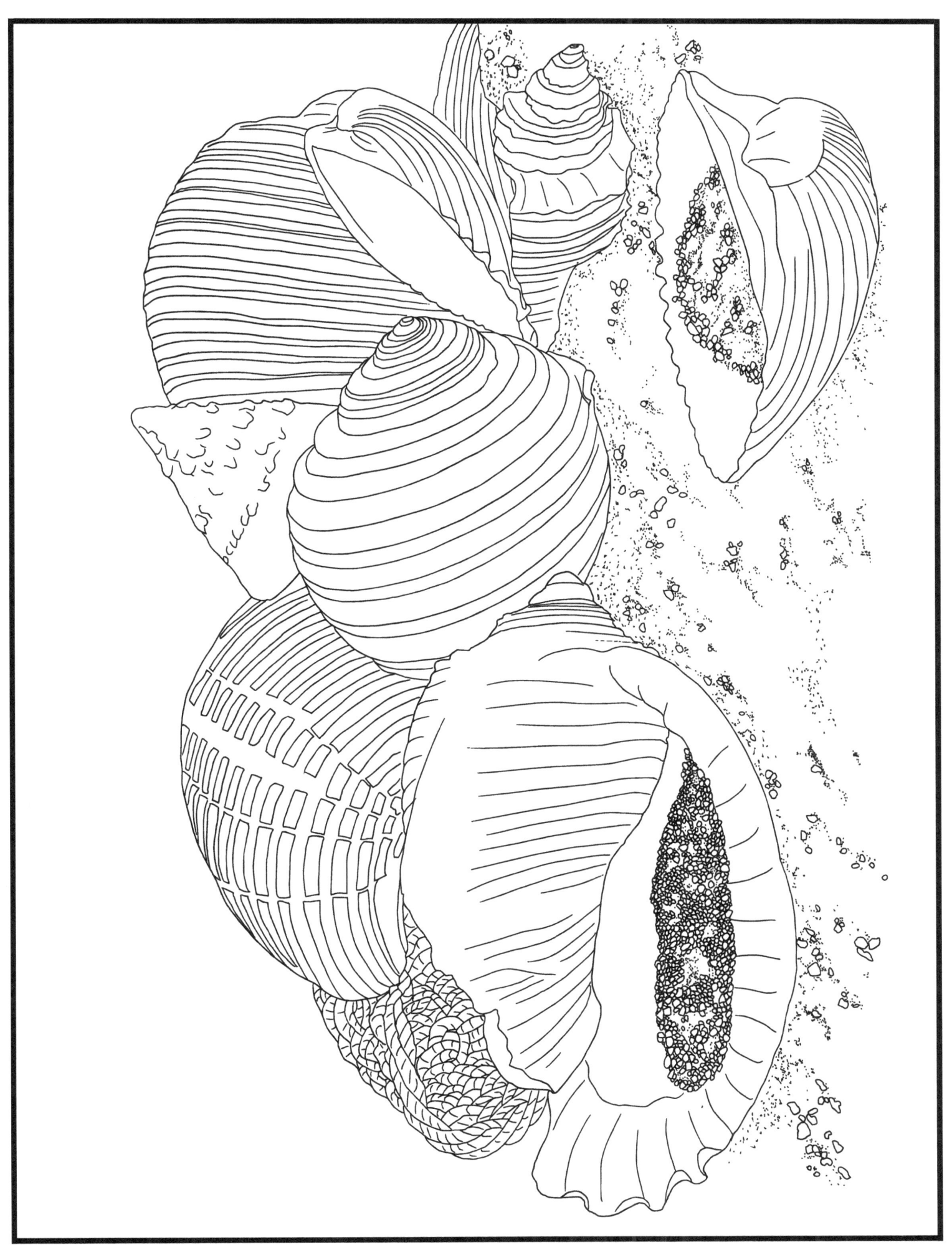

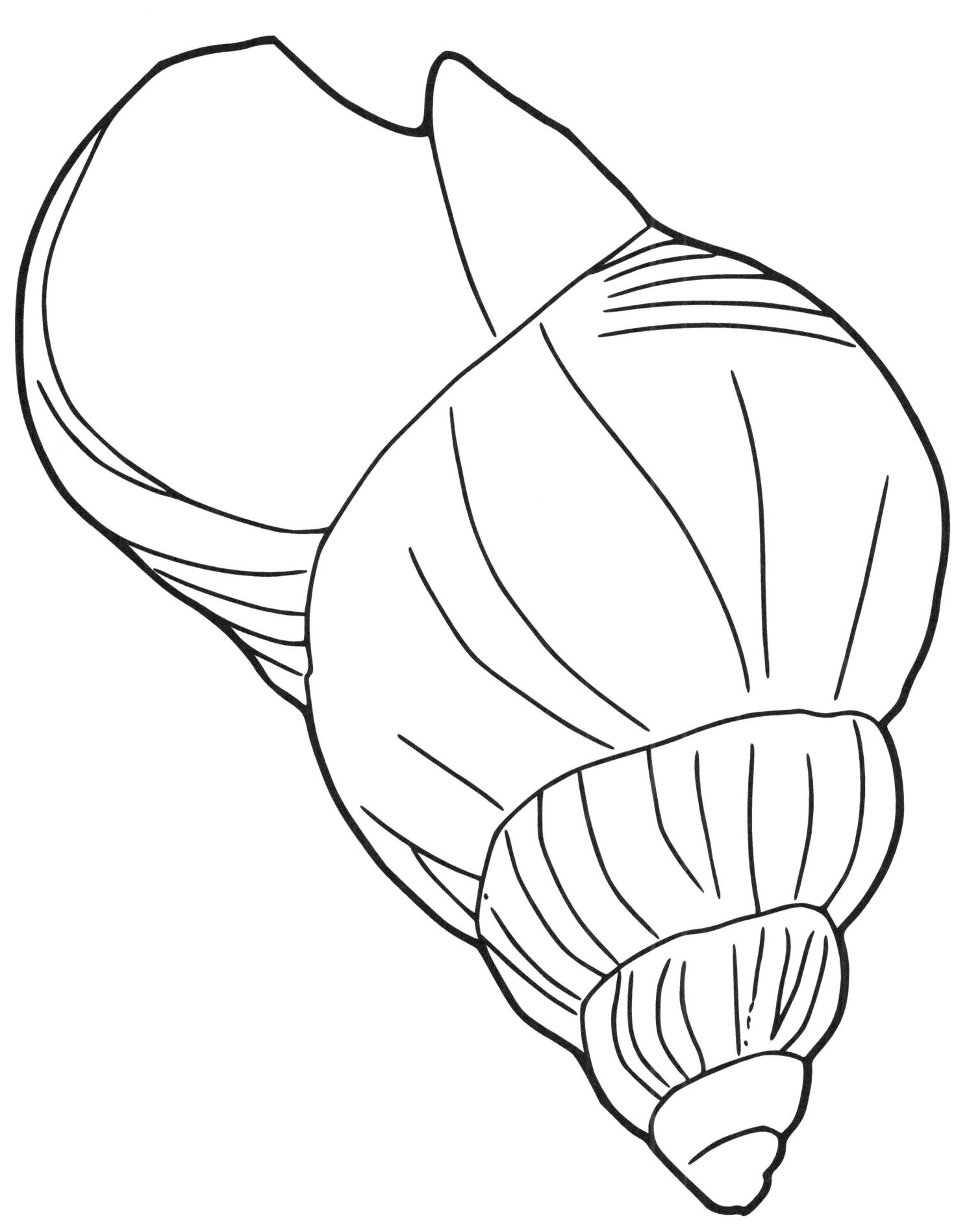

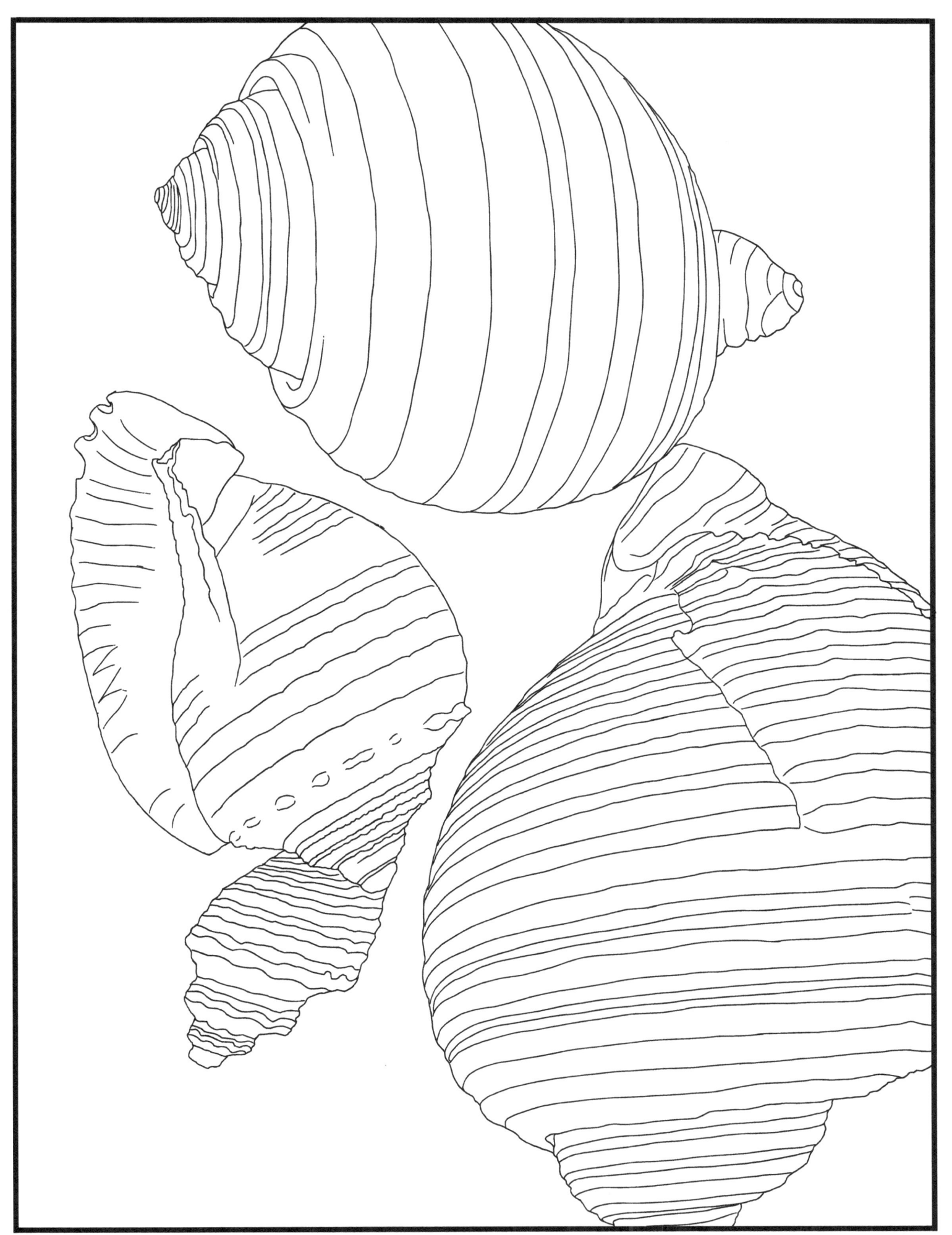

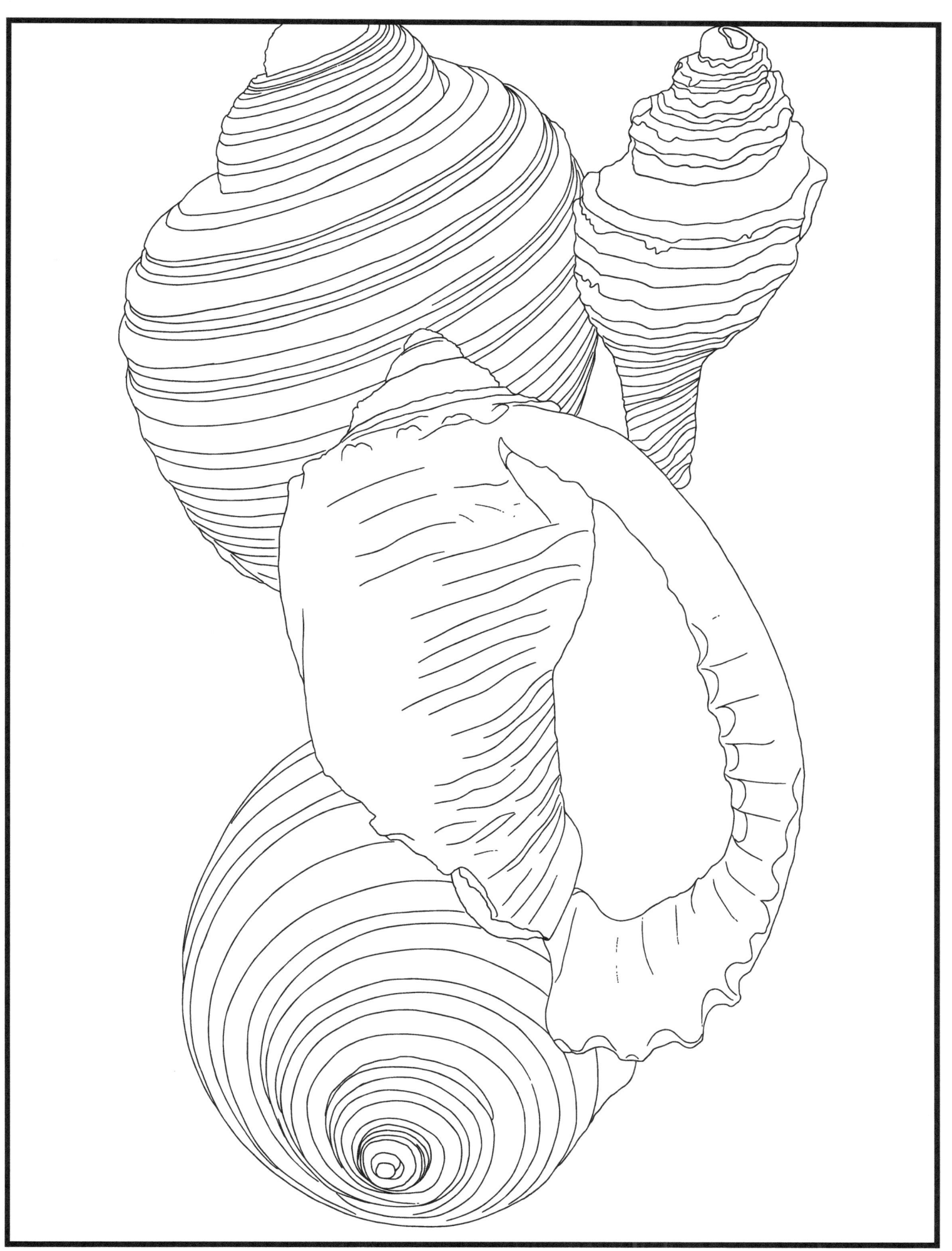

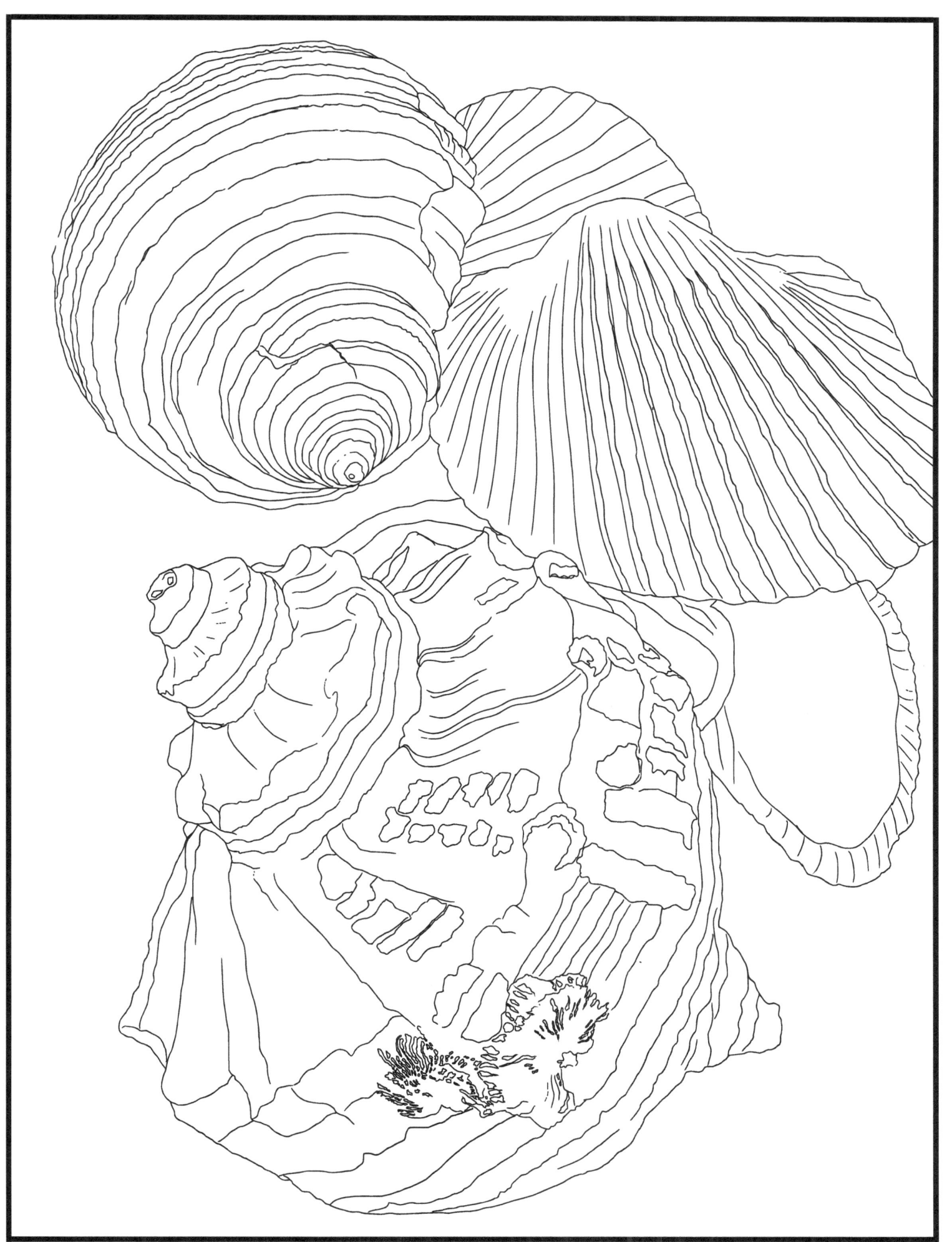

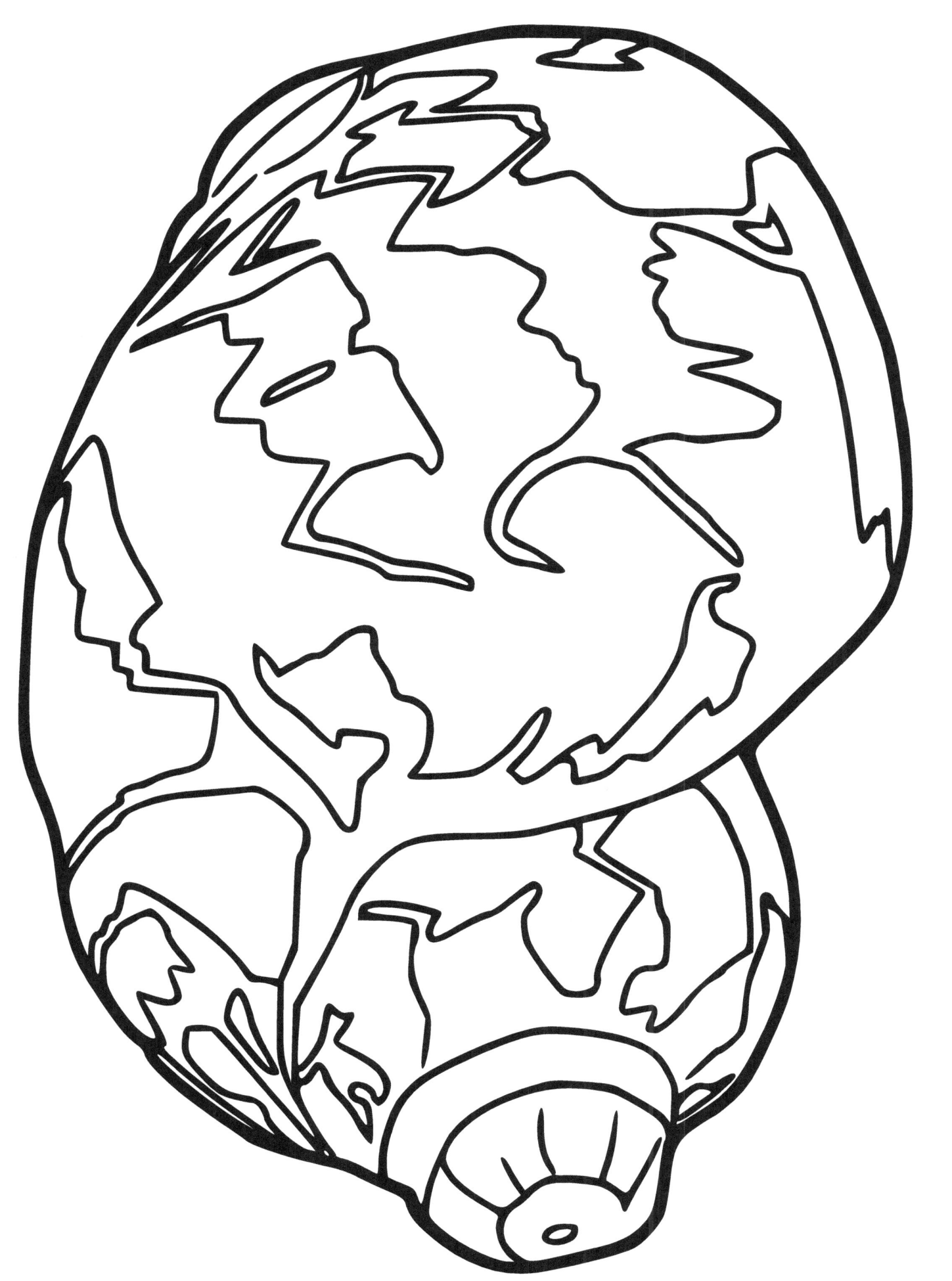

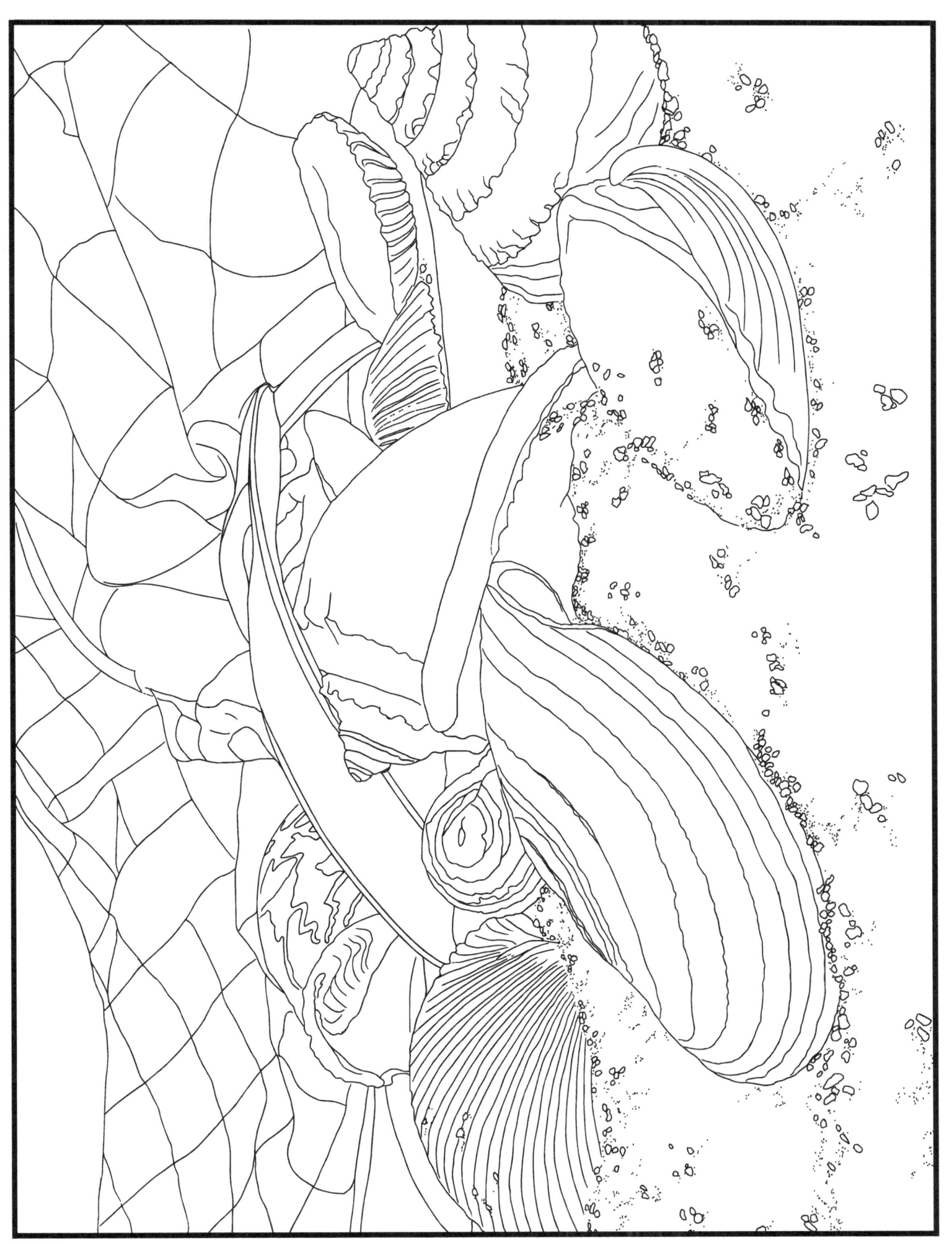

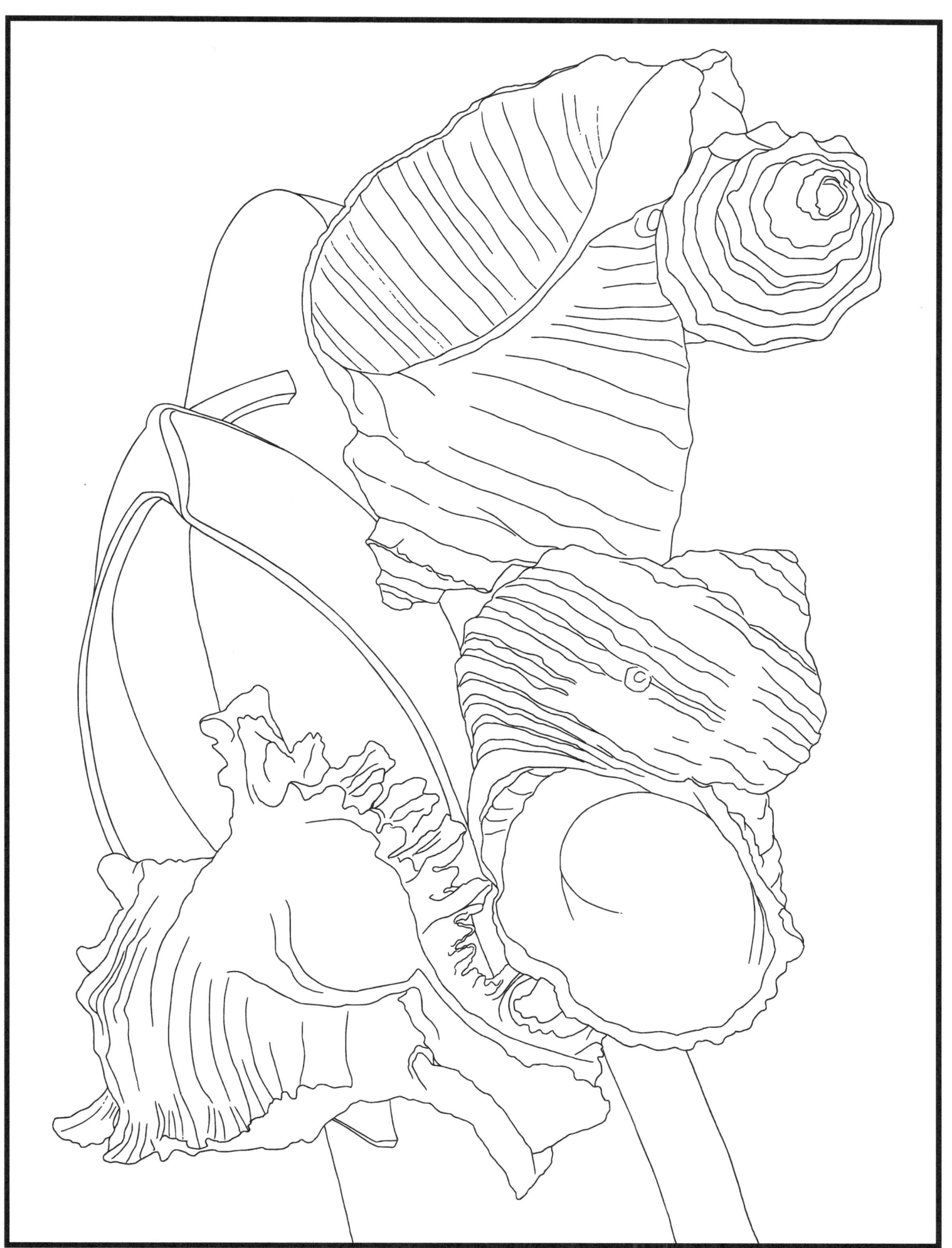

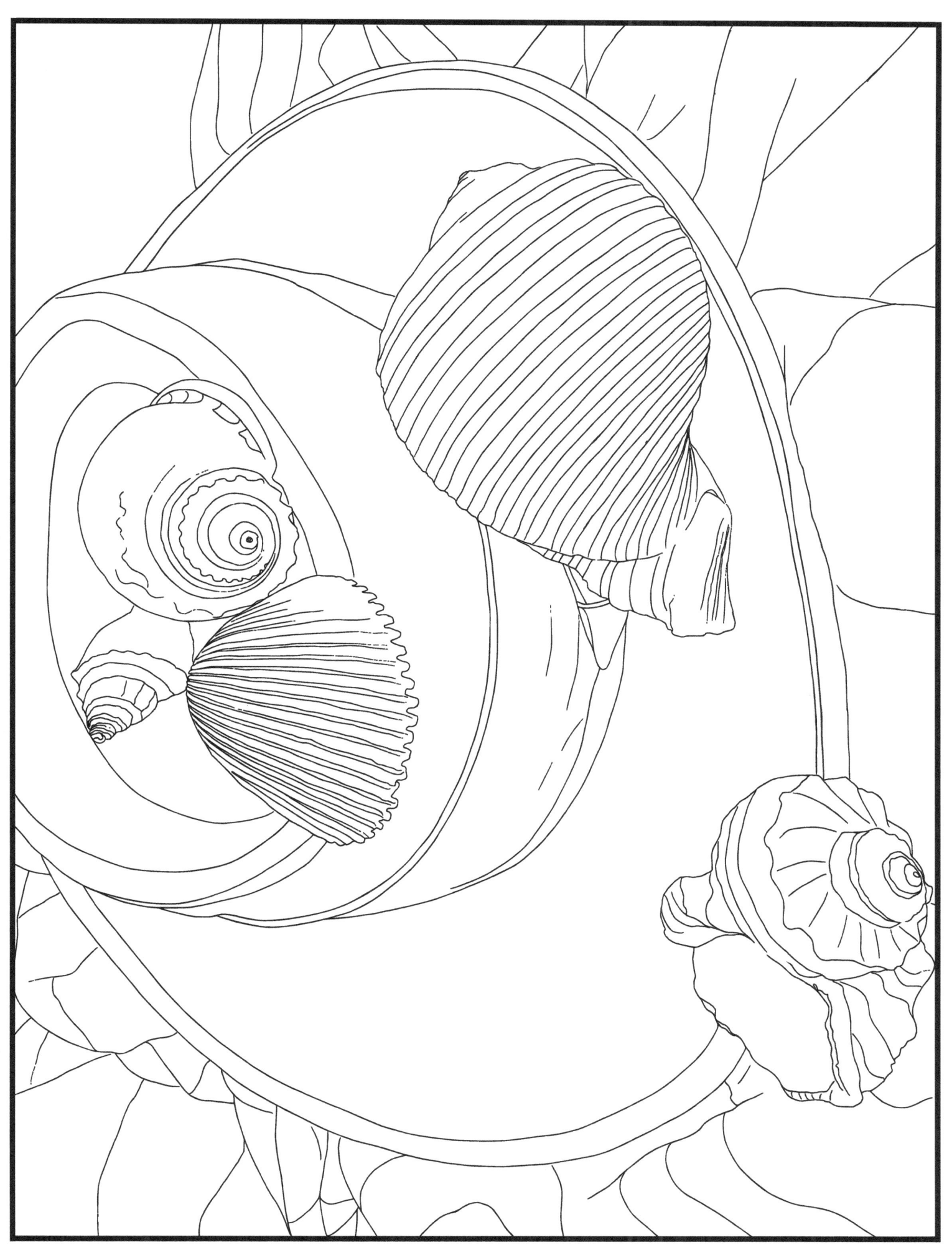

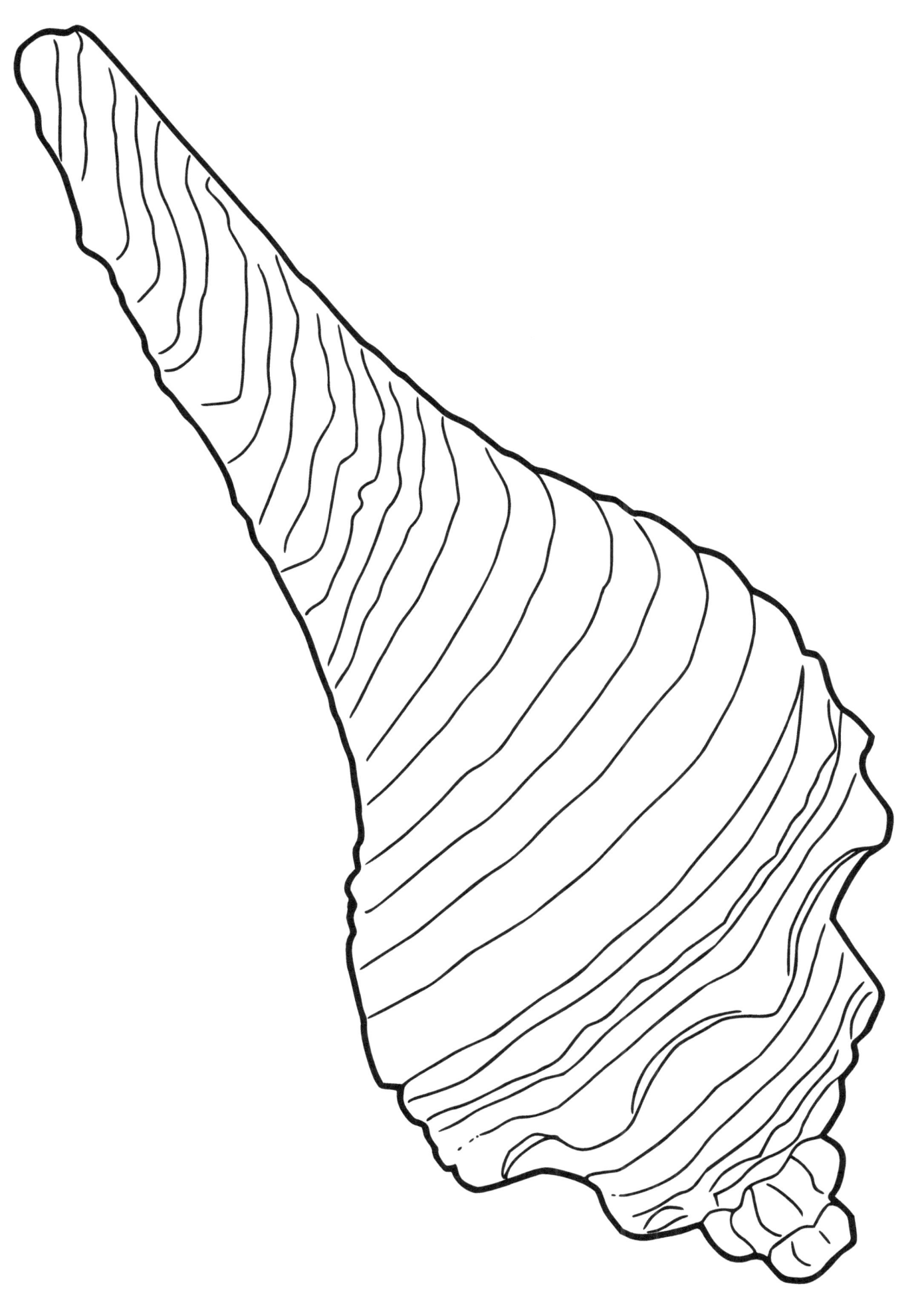

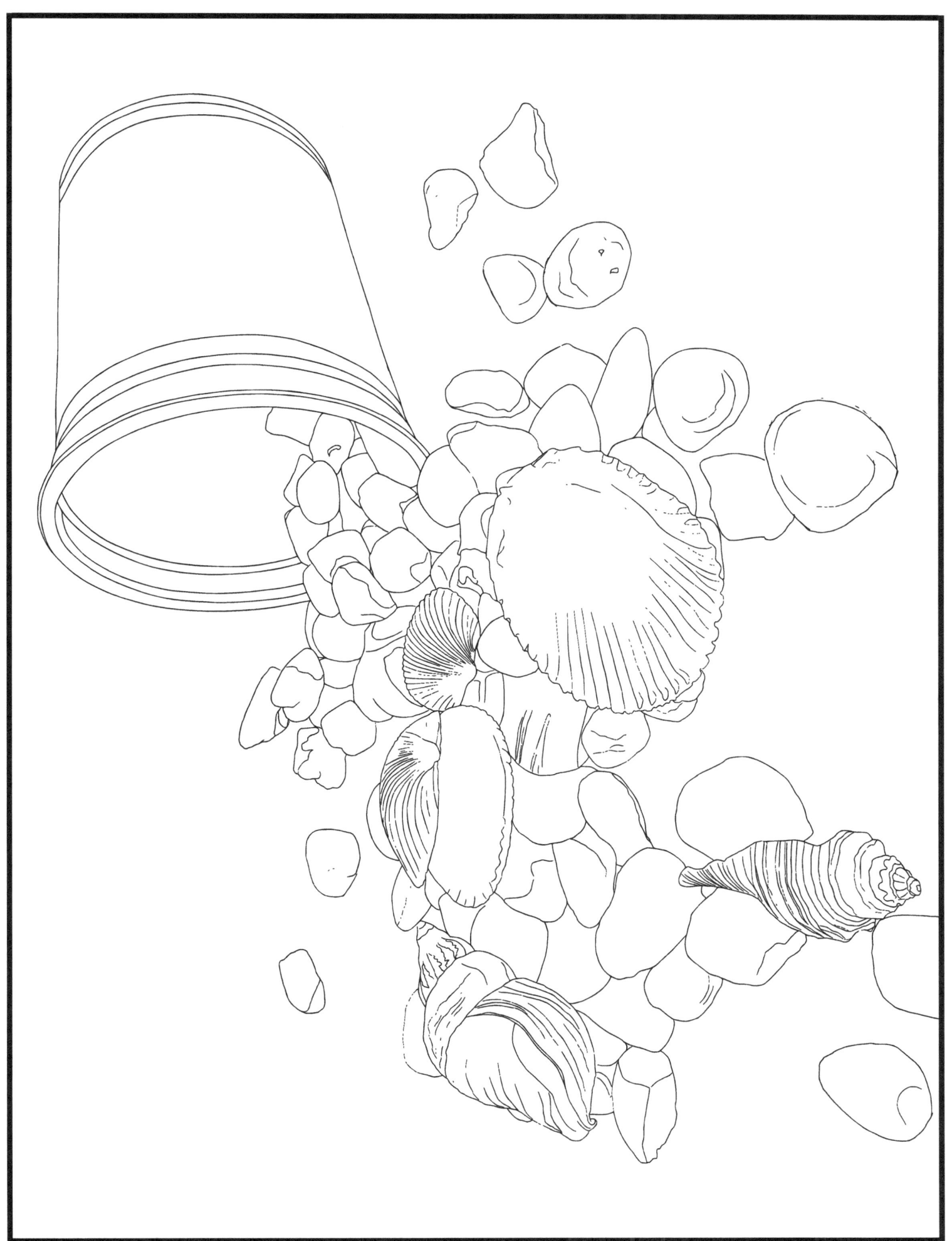

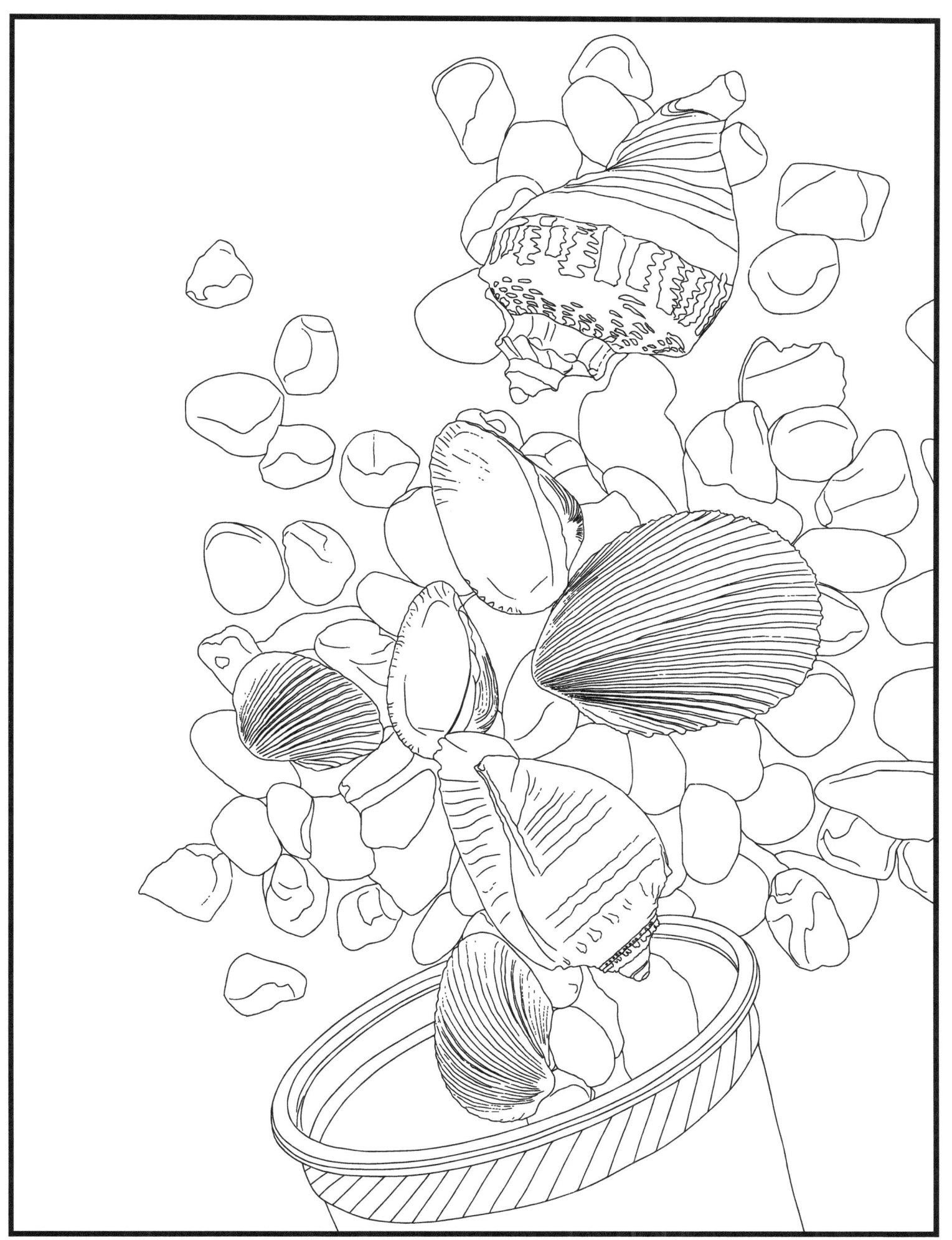

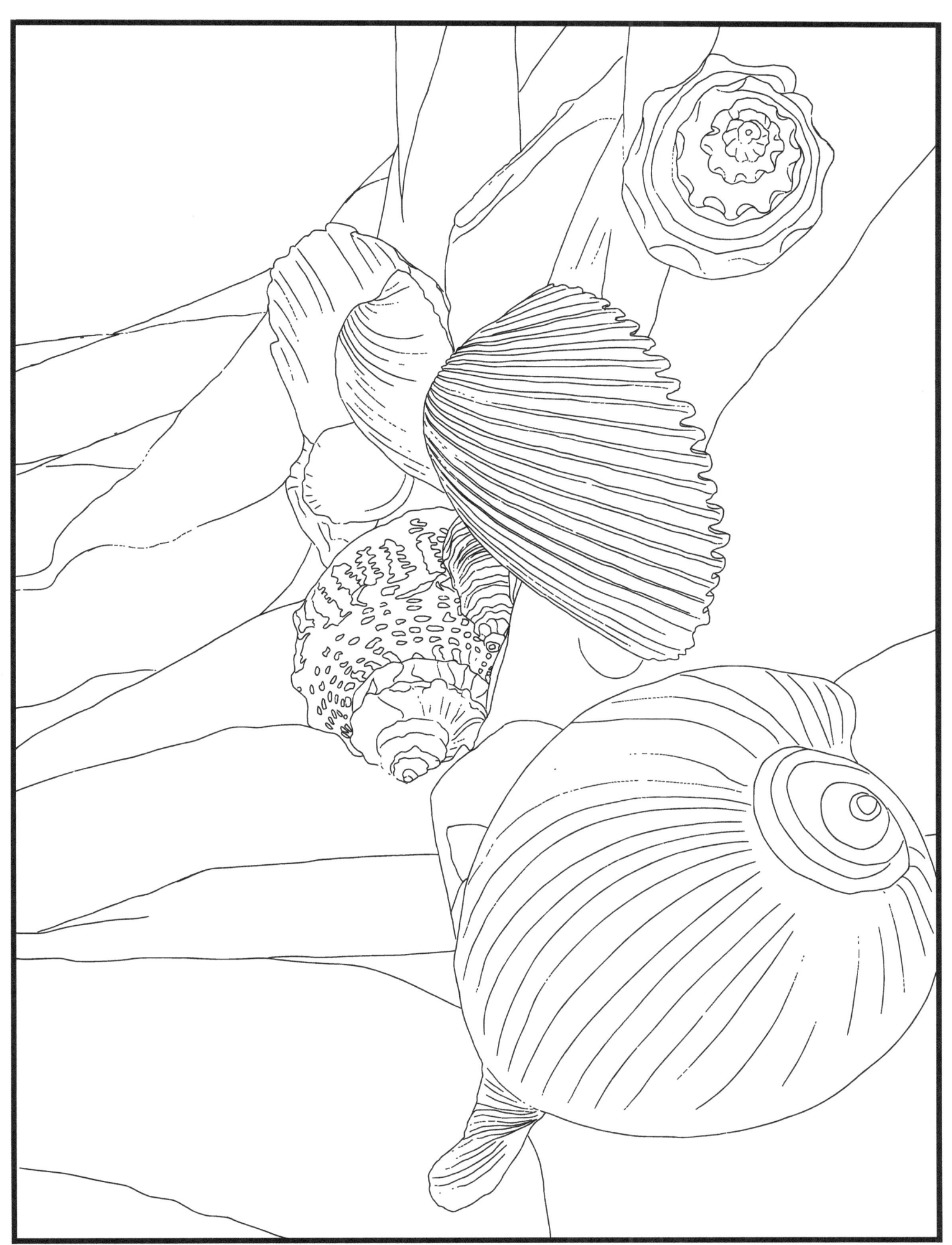

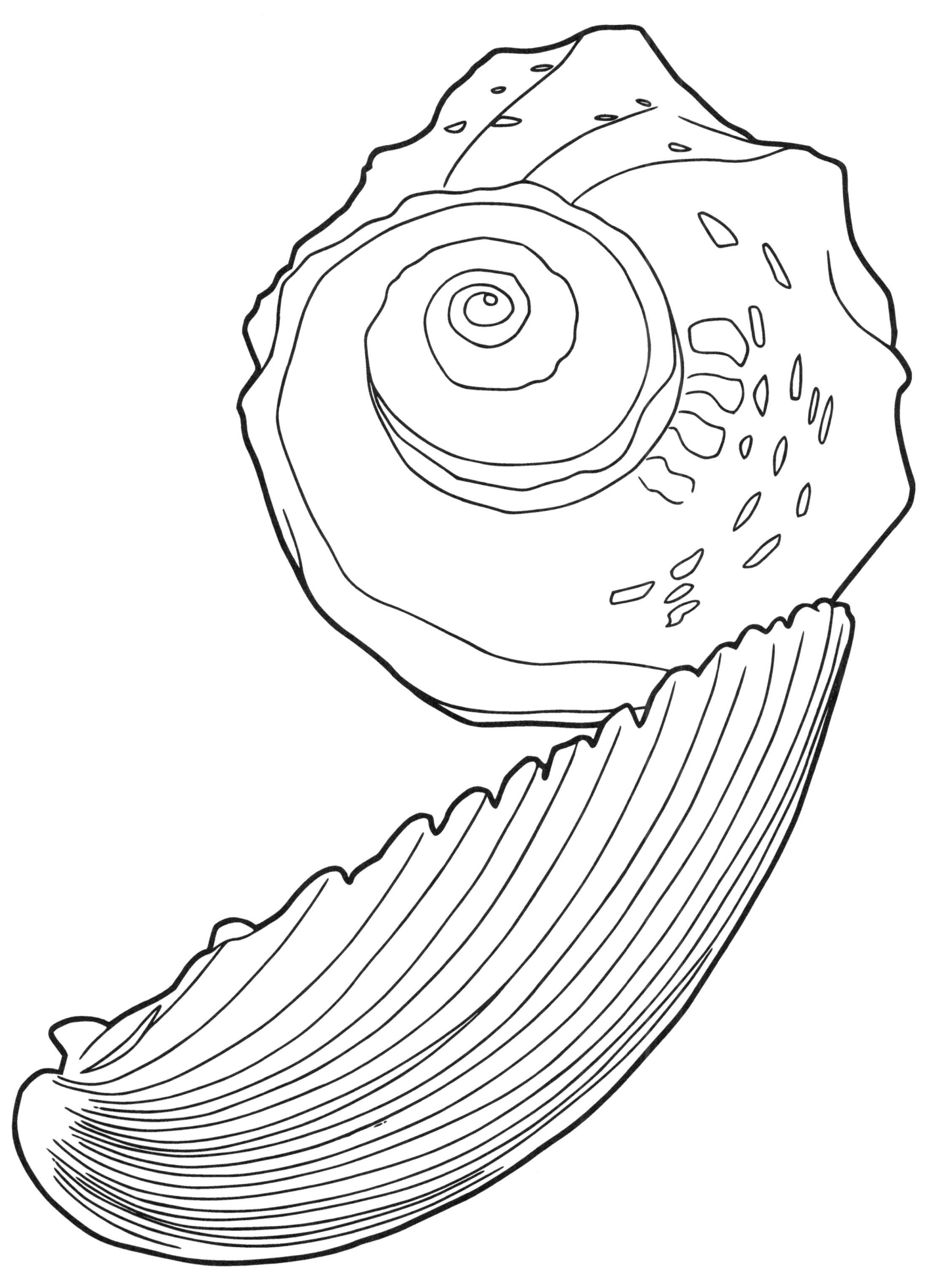

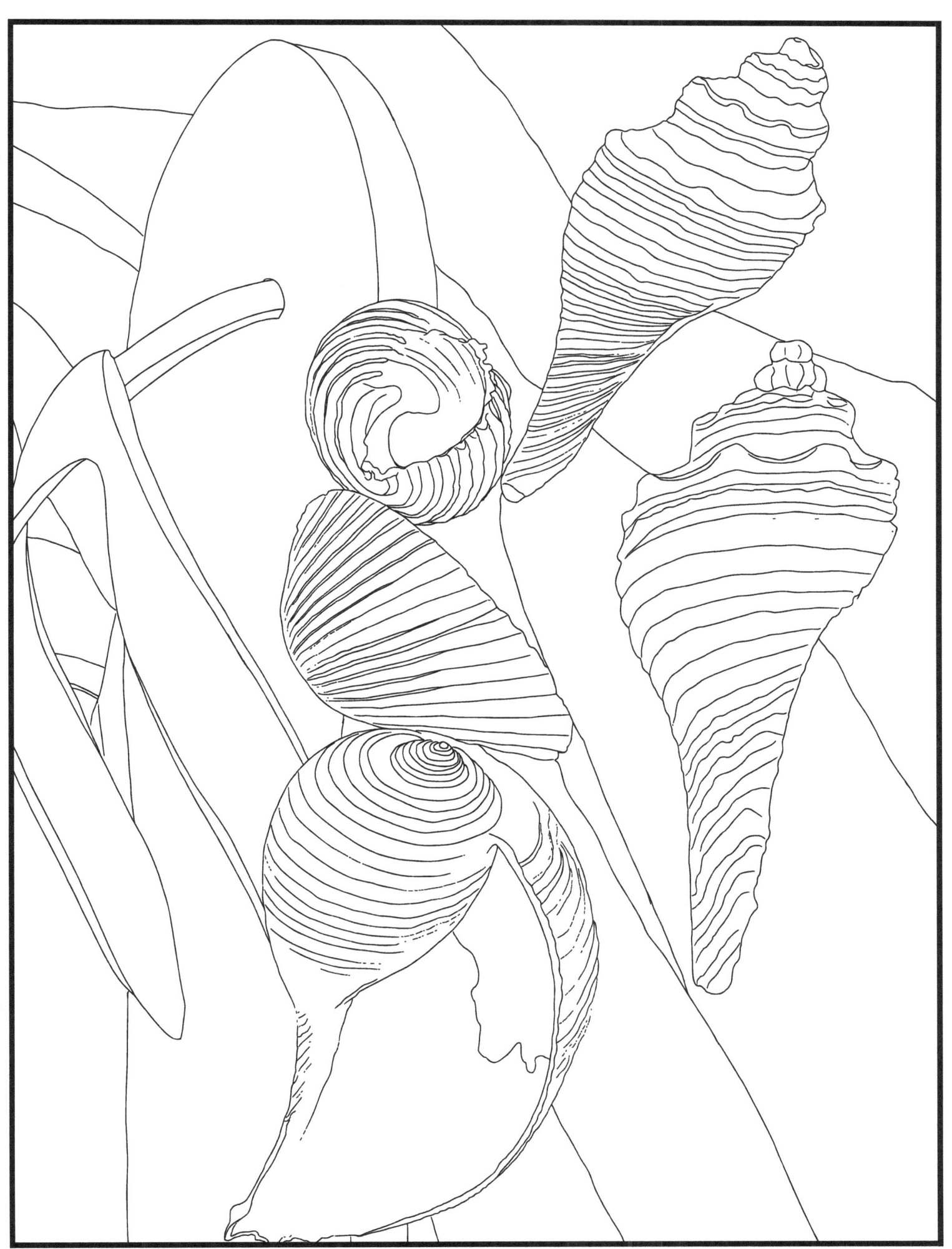

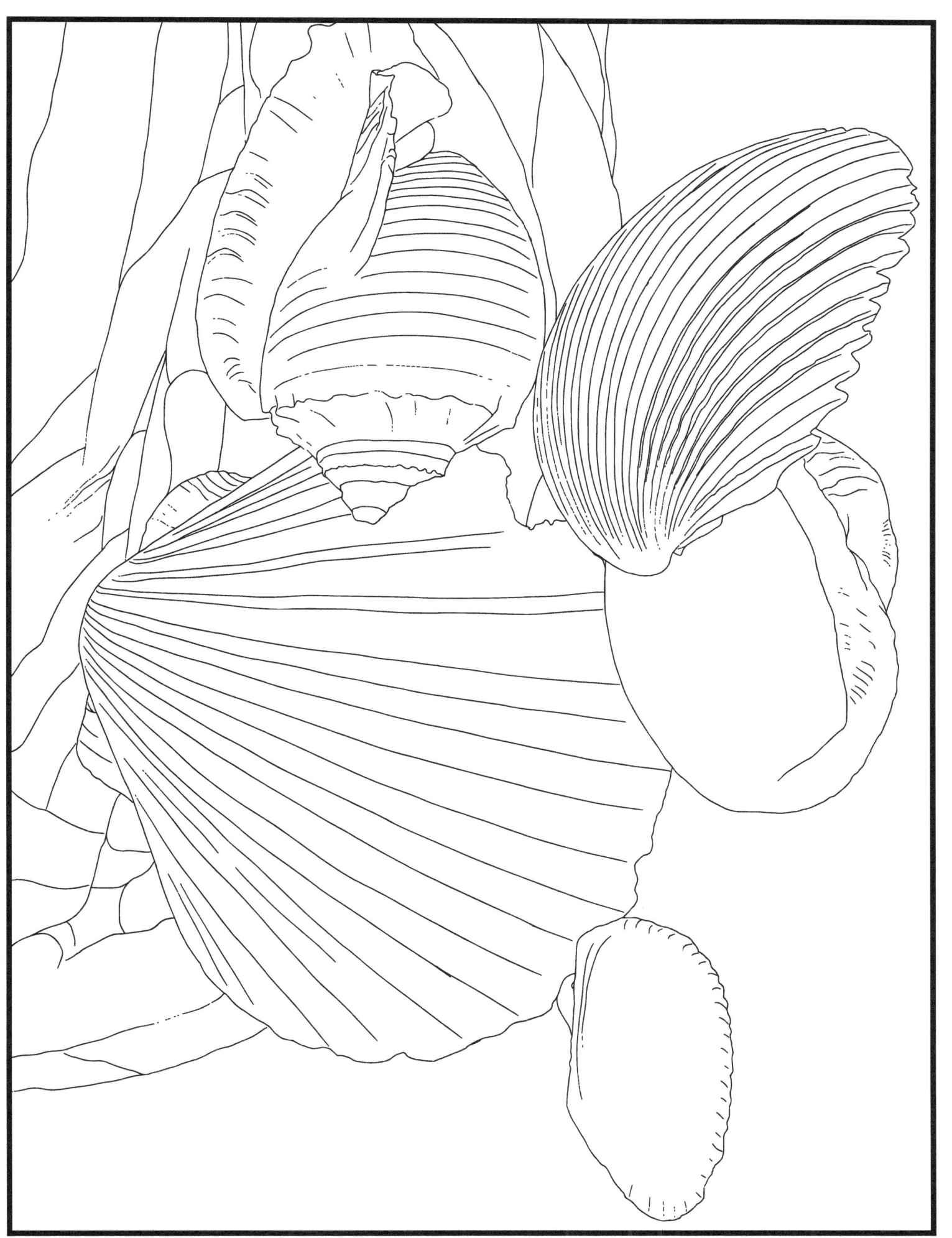

Color Test Page

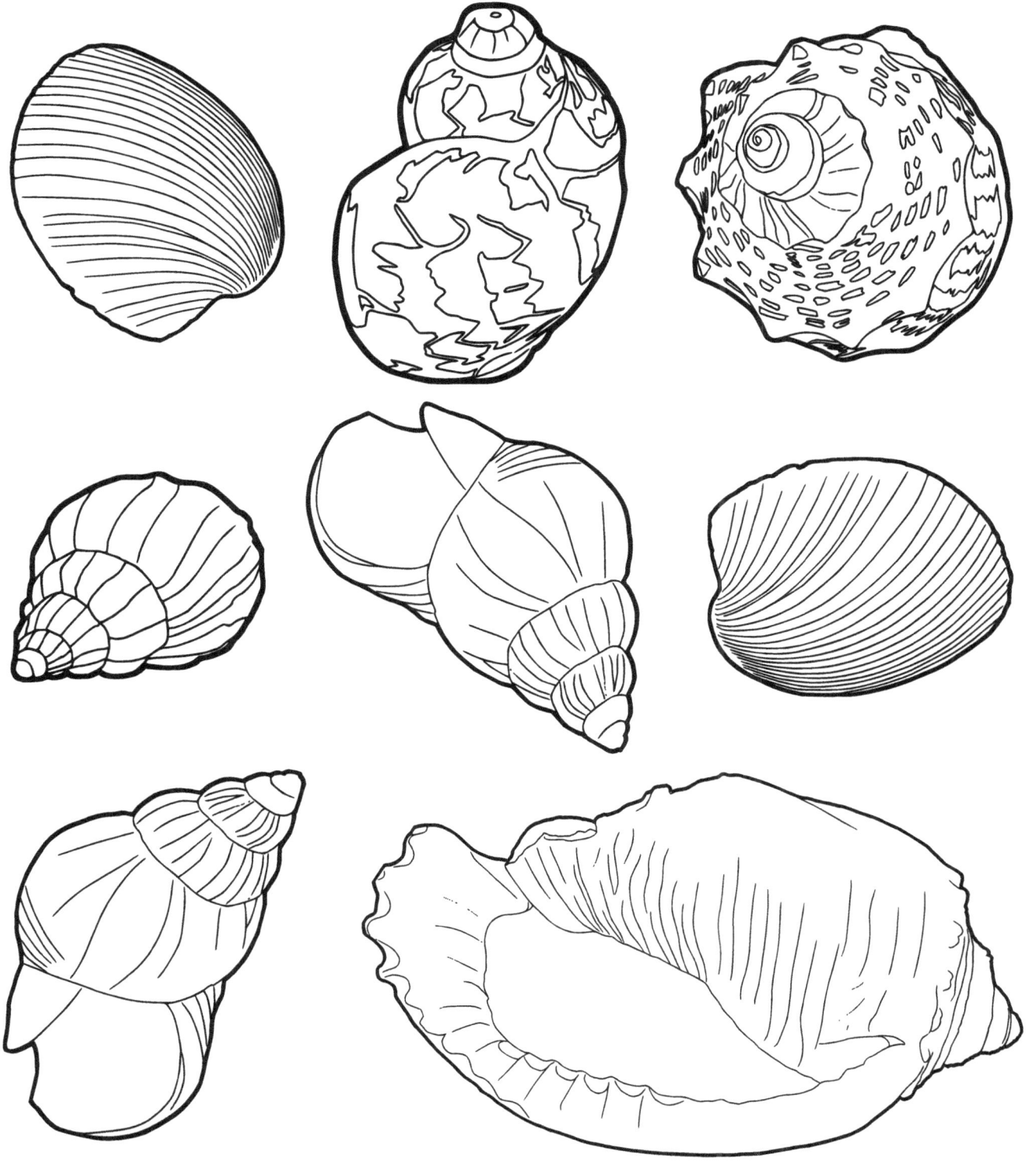

www.ingramcontent.com/pod-product-compliance
Lightning Source LLC
Chambersburg PA
CBHW081633220526
45468CB00009B/2412